THE BLESSED HOPE
AND THE TRIBULATION

THE BLESSED HOPE
AND THE TRIBULATION

A Biblical and Historical Study
of Posttribulationism

by

John F. Walvoord

ZONDERVAN
PUBLISHING HOUSE   OF THE ZONDERVAN CORPORATION
GRAND RAPIDS, MICHIGAN 49506

THE BLESSED HOPE AND THE TRIBULATION

Copyright © 1976 by The Zondervan Corporation
Grand Rapids, Michigan

Library of Congress Cataloging in Publication Data

Walvoord, John F
  The blessed hope and the tribulation.

  Bibliography: p.
  Includes indexes.
    1. Tribulation (Christian eschatology)   2. Rap-
ture (Christian eschatology)   3. Second Advent.
    I. Title
BT888.W34   236'.9   76-13467

Contents

Introduction

1 The Rise of Posttribulational Interpretation 11

2 Classic Posttribulational Interpretation 21

3 Semiclassic Posttribulational Interpretation 31

4 Futurist Posttribulational Interpretation 40

5 Dispensational Posttribulational Interpretation . 60

6 Posttribulational Denial of Imminency and Wrath 70

7 Do the Gospels Reveal a Posttribulational Rapture? ... 82

8 The Comforting Hope of 1 Thessalonians 4 94

9 The Rapture and the Day of the Lord in
   1 Thessalonians 5 108

10 Is the Tribulation Before the Rapture in
   2 Thessalonians? 122

11 The Rapture in Relation to Endtime Events 130

12 Unresolved Problems of Posttribulationism 144

13 Pretribulationism as the Alternative to
   Posttribulationism 159

Bibliography

Subject Index

Scripture Index

Acknowledgments

Unless otherwise indicated, Scripture quotations are from the *King James Version*. Other versions cited are —

—*New International Version, New Testament*. Copyright © 1973 by New York International Bible Society.

—*Revised Standard Version*. Copyright © 1946, 1952 by the Division of Christian Education of the National Council of Churches of Christ in the United States of America.

—*New American Standard Bible*. Copyright © 1960, 1962, 1963, 1968, 1971 by The Lockman Foundation

Introduction

Current events in the world have directed attention as never before to the question of what the future holds for the world, for the church, and for Israel. In this context it is only natural that renewed attention should be given to the blessed hope of Christ's return for His church, and more particularly to the question as to whether believers in Christ can expect momentarily the return of the Lord.

In the theological world, however, almost complete confusion reigns in the interpretation of prophecy. The majority of the church following amillennial interpretation continues to ignore the signs of the times. Among premillenarians a wide variety of views can be found, varying from the extreme of date-setting on the one hand to discounting any imminent hope of the Lord's return on the other. In such a matrix, the question as to whether the church, the body of Christ, will go through the tribulation again becomes acute.

Four different views of the rapture have been advanced and include what is known as midtribulationism and the partial-rapture theory. The major dispute, however, is between pretribulationists and posttribulationists, who debate the question as to whether the church must go through the tribulation before the rapture when the living church will be translated and the dead in Christ resurrected.

Worthy scholars may be found on both sides of this question. Generally speaking, the strategy of posttribulationists has been to attack the pretribulational point of view with the premise that if they can successfully dispose of the pretribulational arguments, posttribulationism will thereby be established. Pretribulationists usually have set forth the reasons for their particular view and have defended it against posttribulational attacks. Posttribulationism, however, has seldom not been subjected to the searching question as to whether it has actually established its own point of view.

It is the purpose of this study to examine the claims of posttribulationists, their exegesis of important passages, and their handling of pretribulational arguments. It soon becomes apparent that posttribulationism is not a single school of thought such as generally characterizes pretribulationism. Posttribulationism actually includes a wide diversity of theological arguments and premises. While a pretribulationist necessarily must be a premillenarian who interprets prophecy literally and has a high regard for the accuracy and authority of Scripture, a posttribulationist could be an amillenarian, a liberal, or a conservative premillenarian.

In this study the amillennial and liberal points of view have been largely ignored, and attention has been directed particularly to posttribulationism as it is found within premillennial interpretation. In premillennial posttribulationism, however, it soon becomes apparent that there are different schools of thought which are conflicting and contradictory.

Four schools of thought within posttribulationism are considered in this study. An attempt will be made to present both the strengths and weaknesses of each school with attention also to the logical inconsistencies which often appear in their arguments. In general, pretribulationists are critical of posttribulationists in three major areas.

First, posttribulationists vary greatly in their doctrine of Scripture. Practically all scholars who deny the inerrancy of the Bible are posttribulationists. By contrast, a pretribulationist by the nature of his argument accepts the authority and accuracy of the Bible. In the discussion in this book, however, this defect in posttribulationism is not treated, as the posttribulational views discussed usually are based on an authoritative Bible.

Second, posttribulationists differ widely in their principles of interpretation. Amillenarians, who are always posttribulational, tend to spiritualize prophecy to such an extent that their posttribulationism is invariably based upon such a spiritualization. It is for this reason that amillenarians seldom debate this question. In premillennial circles it is also a major problem that posttribulationists do not agree among themselves on principles of interpretation of prophecy, for all posttribulationists, to some extent, spiritualize prophetic Scriptures as they relate to the doctrine of the rapture. Even posttribulationists like Robert Gundry who attempt to follow a literal interpretation of prophecy tend to spiritualize any prophecy which would imply pretribulationism.

Third, one of the most critical problems in posttribulationism is its improper use of the inductive method of logic. As theology is largely an inductive science, its doctrinal conclusions are based upon particulars found in the exegesis of relative Scriptures. As the discussion will demonstrate, posttribulationism tends to select certain facts in a given passage and ignores evidence contradictory to its conclusion. Because all the facts are not taken into consideration, its conclusions become faulty logically. Pretribulationists hold that posttribulationism is based either on wrong principles of interpretation or improper logic or both. In brief, posttribulationists are not consistent in interpreting prophecy in its normal or literal sense and violate the principles of inductive logic in selecting only such facts as support their position while ignoring contradictory evidence. The evidence for this will be brought out in the discussion of various aspects of posttribulationism.

It is hoped that this study of posttribulationism will serve to clarify the issues and to provide a better understanding of the conclusion of many specialists in prophecy, namely, that pretribulationism is the most satisfactory view when all facts are taken into consideration. Many believe that the fulfillment of the hope of the Lord's return for His church is imminent and will occur before the final great event of the endtimes, described in the Bible as the great tribulation.

The issue of whether the church will go through the tribulation or be raptured before this time of unprecedented trouble is more than a theological argument. For many pretribulationists the hope of the Lord's return is a very precious truth. To the degree that they long for the coming of the Lord and their gathering unto Him as the beginning of their blessed experience of being forever with the Lord, so proportionately is their disappointment at the possible prospect of a great tribulation, martyrdom, and death. It would be difficult to present a greater contrast between the blessed hope of the imminent return of Christ and the prospect of probable suffering and death in the great tribulation. Accordingly, the argument between pretribulationists and posttribulationists, while determined by the facts of divine revelation, involves an emotional element. The alternatives are drastically different, and with the difference comes a dramatically contrasted future. The claim of some posttribulationists that the difference in point of view is only nominal is not supported by the sharp contrast in eschatological outlook afforded by posttribulationism and pretribulationism.

Those desiring an overall view of the problem — including consideration of midtribulationism and the partial-rapture theory, as well as the arguments supporting pretribulationism — will find these subjects treated in an earlier work by the author, *The Rapture Question*, published by Zondervan.

Portions of this study were first published in *Bibliotheca Sacra* in a series of articles beginning in January 1975. Acknowledgment is made of permission to use this material in revised form in this book as well as quotations from other copyrighted works.

Chapter 1

The Rise of Posttribulational Interpretation

In the history of the church, systematic theology has been a developing science. With this historical development, controversies in various areas of theology have followed, to some degree, the major divisions of systematic theology. In the early centuries the most important theological controversy related to the Scriptures themselves. Some in the postapostolic period, like the Montanists, claimed to have the same inspiration and authority as the apostles who wrote the Scriptures. The early church quickly recognized this as a heresy, and at the Council of Laodicea in 397 the canon was considered closed even though some apocryphal books were later recognized by the Roman Catholic Church.

With the establishment of the Scriptures as the basis of systematic theology, attention soon turned to the doctrine of the Trinity, and the Trinitarian controversies occupied center stage. In 325 the approval of the Nicene Creed, recognizing the full deity of Jesus Christ as a distinct person from the Father, set the stage for recognition of the doctrine of the Trinity as it is normally held in orthodoxy today. It was not until the Council of Constantinople in 381 that the Holy Spirit was given His rightful place. Subsequently the church turned to the doctrine of sins and man, although the outcome was less decisive, as evidenced in the findings of the Council of Orange in 529.

Finally, in the Protestant Reformation, the Augustinian concept of justification by faith was restored. With the withdrawal of the Protestant churches from the Roman Catholic Church, not only was soteriology, the doctrine of salvation by grace, firmly established, but important doctrines related to ecclesiology — such as the priesthood of the believer and the right of every Christian to be his own interpreter of Scripture under the guidance of the Spirit — became cardinal tenets of the Protestant Reformation.

In the history of the church, however, eschatology continued to be an unsettled doctrine. Although the early church for the first two centuries was predominantly chiliastic and held that the second advent of Christ would be followed by a thousand-year reign on earth, this interpretation was soon challenged with the rise of the Alexandrian school of theology in Egypt led by Clement of Alexandria and Origen. An attempt was made to harmonize systematic theology with Platonic philosophy. As this was possible only by interpreting Scripture in a nonliteral sense and regarding Scripture as one great allegory in which the apparent sense was not the real sense, much of the literal meaning of the Scripture was lost, including the doctrine of a literal millennium following the second advent.

The early church, as well as orthodox theologians since, regarded the Alexandrian school as heretical and outside the mainstream of biblical theology. The practical effect of the rise of this school of interpretation, however, was to submerge the premillennial interpretation of Scripture.

Nevertheless, in the fourth and fifth centuries, with Augustine, a consolidation was achieved by separating eschatology from other areas of systematic theology. Two principles of interpretation were adopted by Augustine — a literal, historical, and grammatical interpretation of noneschatological passages,[1] and a nonliteral or figurative interpretation of prophetic Scriptures.[2] The result was that while the Roman Church maintained many of the teachings of the Bible, it continued to use a nonliteral method of interpreting eschatology. Thus amillennialism became the accepted doctrine of the Roman Catholic Church. With the beginning of the Protestant Reformation, the Reformers returned to

Augustine and built on his method of interpretation of prophecy. The Protestant Reformers accordingly were amillennial and opposed premillennialism.

In the aftermath of the Protestant Reformation, with the proliferation of individual churches and denominations, it was only natural that all areas of systematic theology should again be reexamined, including eschatology. Premillennialism, which had formerly included in its ranks some who held extreme views, began to solidify and organize its interpretation of Scripture. This became especially apparent in the last century.

Beginning in the last quarter of the nineteenth century, great prophetic conferences were held, such as the American Bible and Prophetic Conference in America[3] and the Society for the Investigation of Prophecy[4] and Powercourt conferences[5] in the British Isles. Generally speaking, these were sponsored by conservatives in biblical interpretation with the majority promoting premillennialism. Out of this matrix has come a systematic and detailed study of prophecy that has greatly refined the issues and reestablished the doctrine of the second advent of Christ as an important tenet of biblical Christianity. The wide study and discussion of prophecy led to clear understanding of the contrasting views of postmillennialism, premillennialism, and amillennialism.

MAJOR VIEWS OF THE SECOND ADVENT

With the decline of premillennialism after the first two centuries of the early church, amillennialism dominated all major branches of Christianity. Differing explanations were given of prophetic passages that seem to teach premillennialism. The predominant view was that there would be no millennium, or thousand-year reign of Christ, after the second advent, and that the new heavens and the new earth and the eternal state would immediately follow. Passages relating to a kingdom reign of Christ on earth were relegated to the interadvent period and either considered to be a description of the entire period or, as time wore on, of the last thousand years before the second coming of Christ.

In the aftermath of the Protestant Reformation — with the diversity of theological opinion created as Protestantism divided into various denominations and groups — a divergent view of amillennialism known as postmillennialism emerged. Although similar views had been held by various individuals earlier, modern postmillenialism is usually attributed to Daniel Whitby (1638-1726).[6] This new view considered the rise of the church and the preaching of the gospel as eventually being triumphant and ushering in a golden age of a thousand years in which the church throughout the world would flourish. This thousand-year period would climax with the second advent of Christ, much as is taught in amillennialism.

After Whitby, varieties of postmillennialism arose, some being relatively biblical as illustrated in the nineteenth-century theologian, Charles Hodge,[7] and others identifying the optimism of postmillennialism with the organic evolution espoused by liberal theologians such as Albrecht Ritschl,[8] Washington Gladden,[9] and Walter Rauschenbusch.[10] In some cases, postmillennialism became indistinguishable from amillennialism and the terms became almost interchangeable. In general, however, postmillennialism usually adopted a more literal view of the millennium and regarded it as a realistic golden age of spiritual triumph for the church on earth.

During the last century a new variation of doctrine defined the millennial reign of Christ as referring to the intermediate state. This is usually attributed to the Continental theologians Duesterdieck (1859) and Kliefoth (1874).[11] It introduced the new view that the millennium is fulfilled in heaven, not on earth. This interpretation was especially applied to Revelation 20. In the light of various views of amillennialism and postmillennialism, which were evidence of dissatisfaction with these interpretations, premillennialism emerged as a live option.

In the last quarter of the nineteenth century, Darwinian evolution began to penetrate the ranks of postmillenarians. Liberals hailed the theory of evolution, with its easygoing optimism, as the true divine method for bringing in the predicted golden age. Recognizing this as a departure from the faith, more conservative postmillenarians and amillenarians attempted to refute the new evolutionary concept. One of the means used was the calling of great prophetic conferences which were held in the last part of the nineteenth century and continued into the twentieth.

As amillennialism and postmillennialism have little to offer by way of refutation of the concept of evolutionary progress, these prophecy conferences soon became dominated by premillennial interpreters. Many of the doctrines that later became an essential part of premillennial theology were introduced into the discussion, such as the restoration of Israel to the land, a coming time of literal tribulation and trouble on earth, a literal bodily return of Jesus Christ to the earth in His second advent, and a literal kingdom of a thousand years following the second advent. The renewed study of eschatology brought out in the open more than ever before the problem of principles of interpretation of Scripture.

The major question was whether Augustine was right that prophecy should be interpreted in a nonliteral sense. Premillenarians held that the point of departure that had led to amillennialism and postmillennialism was a faulty system of interpretation in which prophecy was made a special case and interpreted in a nonliteral sense. Accordingly they went back to the starting point of the views of the early church fathers, who had been predominantly premillennial, and claimed to be the restorers of the true biblical faith of the early centuries of the church.

THE HERMENEUTICS OF ESCHATOLOGY

The crucial issues that separated premillennialism from amillennialism soon became apparent. The question was whether or not the Bible meant to prophesy literally a restoration of the nation Israel. Was Israel literally once again to return to their ancient land and be restored as a nation? Were the prophecies to be interpreted literally that heresy would increase, that evil would predominate at the end of the age, and that a great tribulation would ultimately emerge?

Most important was the question as to whether the many Old Testament prophecies describing a glorious kingdom on earth, where all nations would be under subjection to Christ and Israel would be prominent as a nation, were destined to be literally fulfilled. Was there to be actually a thousand years during which Christ would reign on earth, beginning with the second advent and the resurrection of saints and climaxing with the divine judgment on rebels? Was Satan actually going to be bound and inactive for the thousand years? If so, the premillenarians claimed, Christ must come before such a thousand-year period rather than at its end. Conservative amillenarians often conceded that if the prophecies were interpreted literally it would lead to such a doctrine, but they continued to insist that prophecy could not be taken literally.

In discussing premillennialism as an emerging doctrine of the church, it is only natural that other questions should be raised, including the relationship of prophecies pertaining to a rapture or translation of the church and the question of where this fits into the prophetic program. Amillenarians and postmillenarians merged this with the second advent of Christ, but a view soon surfaced among premillenarians that the coming of Christ for His church was a distinct event which, as a matter of fact, would occur before the time of great tribulation instead of at its close. Divergent views of pretribulationism and posttribulationism became major issues in prophecy accompanying the new consideration of premillennialism as the proper view.

VARIETIES OF POSTTRIBULATIONISM

In eschatology as a whole as well as in the controversies relating to the place of the rapture of the church in the sequence of events in the prophetic program, posttribulationism continued to be the majority view. It was universally held by liberal theologians, who tended to take prophecy in a nonliteral sense. It also coincided with all forms of postmillennialism and amillennialism, as their principle of interpreting prophecy in a nonliteral sense naturally led to this conclusion. It was only in premillennial interpretation that opposition to posttribulationism arose.

Within posttribulationism, however, a variety of explanations and interpretations have characterized the history of the doctrine. Although the early church in the first two centuries was premillennial, the postapostolic Fathers tended to identify their contemporary persecutions with the great tribulation immediately preceding the second advent. Although they usually linked this with the view that Christ's coming could occur at any time, they do not seem to have contemplated a period between the translation of the church and the second advent of Christ to set up His thousand-year kingdom.[12] Accordingly, although their post-tribulationism is quite different from most forms of post-tribulationism extant, their view of the rapture of the church seems to have combined it with the second advent.

Most of the early church fathers, however, made little effort to refine the doctrine and solve the seeming conflicts of their point of view. The problem of imminency of the rapture when events before the second advent remained unfulfilled does not seem to have caused concern. Quite a few of the early church fathers in the first two centuries were silent on the whole problem, and it does not seem to have been a major issue. With the rise of amillennialism in the third century, there was little incentive to study the problem of posttribulationism, and there was little or no progress in the study of eschatology until the Protestant Reformation.

The Protestant Reformers, returning to Augustine, delivered the church from the doctrines of purgatory and other Roman inventions but do not seem to have raised any questions about the rapture of the church as a separate event. It was only when premillennialism began to demand a literal interpretation of prophecy and reexamine the prophetic program of Israel and other issues that the question began to be raised whether the rapture, as a matter of fact, could be harmonized with the doctrines that declare that Christ will return to set up His kingdom.

In the last century a number of varieties of posttribulationism have emerged, some of them quite recent in their major tenets. In general, they cover the gamut of the possibilities.

J. Barton Payne, in his *Imminent Appearing of Christ*,[13] advocates a return to what he says was the position of the early church, that is, a premillennial and posttribulational point of view which spiritualizes the tribulation and identifies it with the contemporary problems of Christianity. Comparatively few have followed Payne, however, though a tendency to spiritualize the period of tribulation is a general characteristic of posttribulationism.

Alexander Reese, in his *Approaching Advent of Christ*,[14] presented the most comprehensive defense of posttribulationism. His popular form of posttribulationism had as its key doctrine that the church is the true Israel and includes saints of all ages.

Oswald Allis, a prominent amillenarian, also advanced this point of view.[15] Because the Scriptures, even from the premillennial point of view, clearly picture saints or a redeemed people in the period of future tribulation, this form of posttribulationism concludes that it is unquestionably true that the church will go through the tribulation. A variation of this makes both Israel and the church one as a covenant community who share the same eschatology.

Reese's book also offers evidence that the resurrection of the church occurs at the same time as the resurrection of Revelation 20. Major emphasis is placed on terms like "appearing," "the day," "the end," and "revelation" as technical terms that relate the rapture to the second coming as the terminus of the present age. Reese was probably one of the best exponents of posttribulationism, and later writers supporting posttribulationism usually borrow extensively from his arguments.

In posttribulationism it is common to identify the doctrine with orthodoxy because it was held by the Protestant Reformers and the Roman theologian, Augustine. Holding that posttribulationism is the historic position of the church, its advocates label any other view as a departure from historic Christianity.

All the views previously mentioned consider the church already in the tribulation and identify the trials of the church through the centuries as the fulfillment of prophecies of a time of trouble preceding the second advent of Christ.

A futuristic school of interpretation among posttribulationism, however, has also emerged. One of its most prominent adherents is George Ladd whose work, *The Blessed Hope*,[16] promotes the view that the great tribulation is still future. While other views of posttribulationism could conceivably be harmonized with the idea that Christ could return at any moment, Ladd considers it inevitable that at least a seven-year period (described in Dan. 9:27) separates the church today from the rapture and the second advent of Christ which are aspects of the same event. Although Ladd's argument builds largely on the fact of the history of the doctrine and extols posttribulationism as the norm for orthodoxy through the centuries, he introduces a new realism into the picture in adopting a literal future tribulation. His views have been somewhat qualified by his later writings, but in general he seems to retain a futuristic view of the great tribulation with its corresponding doctrine that Christ's return could not be any day, but can only follow the years required to fulfill prophecies relating to the tribulation.

The most recent theory of posttribulationism has been advanced by Robert Gundry in his work *The Church and the Tribulation*.[17] Gundry, following the lead of many premillenarians, distinguishes Israel and the church as separate entities and attempts a literal interpretation of many of the prophecies that deal with the endtimes. In advancing his theory he refutes most of the posttribulationists who have preceded him. Working with these premises, he endeavors to establish a new doctrine of posttribulationism which he tries to harmonize with a literal interpretation of prophecy.

Gundry's work poses a number of theological problems both for other posttribulationists and for contemporary pretribulationists. Because his arguments, in the main, are new and propound a form of posttribulationism never advanced before, his work is a milestone and creates further need for study of posttribulationism in the history of the church. The chapters which follow will attempt to analyze the strengths and weaknesses of these various views of posttribulationism and the arguments advanced in support of conflicting posttribulational interpretations of prophecy.

Notes

[1] Bernard Ramm, *Protestant Biblical Interpretation* (Boston: W. A. Wilde Co., 1950), p. 10.

[2] Oswald T. Allis, *Prophecy and the Church* (Philadelphia: Presbyterian and Reformed Publishing Co., 1945), p. 3.

[3] Nathaniel West, ed., *Premillennial Essays* (New York: Fleming H. Revell Co., 1879).

[4] Ernest R. Sandeen, *The Roots of Fundamentalism* (Chicago: University of Chicago Press, 1970), pp. 22-25.

[5] Ibid., pp. 34-41.

[6] Augustus Hopkins Strong, *Systematic Theology*, 7th ed. (Philadelphia: A. C. Armstrong & Son, 1902), p. 1014.

[7] Charles Hodge, *Systematic Theology*, 3 vols. (New York: Charles Scribner's Sons, 1895), 3:790-880.

[8] Albrecht Ritschl, *The Christian Doctrine of Justification and Reconciliation*, ed.

H. R. Mackintosh and A. B. Macaulay (Clifton, N.J.: Reference Book Publishers. 1966).

[9] Richard D. Knudten, *The Systematic Thought of Washington Gladden* (New York: Humanities Press, 1968), pp. 111-17.

[10] Walter Rauschenbusch, *A Theology for the Social Gospel* (New York: Macmillan Co., 1922), pp. 131-66.

[11] B. B. Warfield, *Biblical Doctrines* (New York: Oxford University Press, 1929), pp. 643-64.

[12] Adolph von Harnack, *History of Dogma*, trans. Neil Buchanan, 7 vols. (New York: Dover Publications, 1961), 1:168.

[13] J. Barton Payne, *The Imminent Appearing of Christ* (Grand Rapids: Wm. B. Eerdmans Publishing Co., 1962).

[14] Alexander Reese, *The Approaching Advent of Christ* (London: Marshall, Morgan & Scott, 1937).

[15] Allis, *Prophecy and the Church.*

[16] George E. Ladd, *The Blessed Hope* (Grand Rapids: Wm. B. Eerdmans Publishing Co., 1956).

[17] Robert H. Gundry, *The Church and the Tribulation* (Grand Rapids: Zondervan Publishing House, 1973).

Chapter 2

Classic Posttribulational Interpretation

Posttribulationists are united in refutation of pretribulationism, midtribulationism, and the partial-rapture view, but within posttribulationism itself at least four distinct schools of thought have emerged in the twentieth century. Although it is difficult to name them accurately, they can be denominated (1) classic posttribulationism; (2) semiclassic posttribulationism; (3) futuristic posttribulationism; (4) dispensational posttribulationism. Because classic posttribulationism is rooted most deeply in the history of the church and depends in large degree on the validity of the eschatology of the early church, it is the natural starting point in considering the varied and somewhat contradictory approaches to posttribulationism advanced today.

Probably the most vocal, scholarly, and effective exponent of classic posttribulationism is J. Barton Payne. In a recent publication Payne has called his view "pasttribulation," because according to his point of view, the great tribulation is already past, fulfilled in history, and hence Christ's coming could be any moment.[1] Dr. Payne has also written a recent major work on prophecy, *Encyclopedia of Biblical Prophecy*,[2] which has been considered by some a major contribution to contemporary interpretation. His earlier work, *The Imminent Appearing of Christ*,[3] delineates in specific form his concept of classic posttribulationism. Payne reacts against George Ladd's concept of a future tribulation presented in *The Blessed Hope*[4] and this author's *The Rapture Question*,[5] which defends pretribulationism. Although in the main a refutation of pretribulationism, Payne's work relies for its conclusions in large measure on his definition, support, and defense of classic posttribulationism. His point of view may be summarized under four propositions which form the basis of this discussion: (1) the imminency of the second coming; (2) the posttribulational second coming; (3) a nonliteral tribulation preceding the second coming; (4) a literal millennium following the second coming.

The Second Coming as an Imminent Event

Payne's belief in the imminency of Christ's return is his major contribution to posttribulationism. By "imminency" he means that the rapture of the church and the second coming of Christ to the earth could occur any day at any moment. He summarizes his view in these words:

> Finally, the "blessed hope," as it has been interpreted by the classical view of the church, is one the full accomplishment of which is imminent. Each morning, as the Christian casts his glance into the blueness of the sky, he may thrill with the prayerful thought, "Perhaps today!" Or, if his particular skies be shrouded in gloom, still the blackest moment comes just before the dawn. His very prayer of petition may be cut short by "a great earthquake" (Rev. 6:12). Then, "Look up, and lift up your heads; because your redemption draweth nigh" (Luke 21:28).[6]

Having defined imminency as the possibility of Christ's return any day, Payne offers further explanation of his concept of imminency in the third chapter of his work. Here he states, "The term 'imminent' applies to an event 'almost always of danger,' which is 'impending threateningly; hanging over one's head; ready to befall or overtake one; close at hand in its incidence; coming on shortly.' "[7] After citing Matthew 24:38-39, 42; 25:13; Revelation 22:7,12; as compared to Revelation 3:11; 22:20, he states, "It should therefore be clear at the outset that imminency does not mean that Christ's coming *must* be soon. . . . The day of Christ's appearing rests in the hands of God, 'which in its own times *he* shall show' (1 Tim. 6:15)."[8] Payne adds, "Does this mean then that it could be so soon as to happen right away, at any time? This is the thought that is associated with imminency, 'ready to befall or overtake one'; and the question of biblical eschatology is whether such a possibility does actually characterize Christ's second advent."[9]

In his historical introduction to the subject of the appearing of Christ, Payne quotes the ante-Nicene fathers to support his view that the early church held to the doctrine of imminency. He states, "Prior to the Council of Nicaea in A.D. 325, the ancient church was characterized in general by two convictions respecting the sequence of events of Christ's second coming."[10] Payne summarizes these two convictions as follows: "The ante-Nicene fathers thus held two basic convictions relative to the second coming of Christ: that it was imminent, and that it was post-tribulational."[11]

In support of the concept of imminency he states, "In the first place, it expected that the Lord could appear in the clouds in immediate connection with any day of contemporary life. The ante-Nicene fathers, in other words, were committed to the concept of the imminence of their Lord's return."[12] Payne qualifies this, however, with the statement, "It must be observed at the outset, however, that imminency as herein defined does not mean that it *had* to be close at hand, only that it *could* be, that the establishment of Christ's eschatological kingdom was conceived of as capable of overtaking them at any time."[13]

Payne cites the *First Epistle of Clement*, the *Epistle of Barnabas*, the *Epistle of Ignatius to the Ephesians* and Ignatius in *Epistle to Polycarp* and other early fathers on imminency.[14] In general, Payne establishes the fact that at least some of the early fathers expected the return of Christ momentarily even though how soon it might occur is not always clear. Whether or not all actually believed Christ could come any day, the extent of the evidence is that they commonly did expect Christ's coming soon, and a recurring note is the thought that they were in the very last days.

With the advent of the Alexandrian school of theology about A.D. 200 and its attack on the literalness of prophecy in general the hope of imminency receded. Payne states, "Although the entire body of the early fathers, insofar as they expressed themselves, held to the above-outlined position of imminent post-tribulationism, there did appear, beginning at the close of the second century among the apologists who succeeded the apostolic fathers, a few exceptions."[15] As the church drifted into amillennialism, especially following Augustine, the doctrine of imminency became obscure. Payne concludes, "By medieval times there was thus exhibited a considerable deviation from the original expectancy of the imminent appearance of Christ."[16]

THE CLASSIC VIEW THAT THE SECOND COMING IS POSTTRIBULATIONAL

As already indicated, the classic view of posttribulationism states that the early church held the second coming of Christ to be not only imminent, but posttribulational. The preponderance of evidence seems to support the concept that the early church did not clearly hold to a rapture as preceding the endtime tribulation period. Most of the early church fathers who wrote on the subject at all considered themselves already in the great tribulation. Accordingly Payne, as well as most other posttribulationists, takes the position that it is self-evident that pretribulationism as it is taught today was unheard of in the early centuries of the church. Consequently the viewpoint of the early church fathers is regarded by practically all posttribulationists, whether adherents of the classic view or not, as a major argument in favor of posttribulationism. However, the fact that most posttribulationists today do not accept the doctrine of imminency as the early church held it diminishes the force of their argument against pretribulationism.

Most posttribulationists today actually reject the posttribulationism of the early church fathers. Payne stands almost alone in his strict adherence to the viewpoint of the early church on prophecy. Not only have all amillenarians rejected the prophetic outlook of the early church, but most premillenarians also believe that the early church was mistaken when they considered themselves already in the great tribulation.

Generally speaking, however, Payne has correctly analyzed the writings of the early church fathers in assuming that they should be classified as posttribulational. While the force and cogency of this point of view may be debated, the historical fact is that the early church fathers' view on prophecy did not correspond to what is advanced by pretribulationists today except for the one important point that both subscribe to the imminency of the rapture.

THE CLASSIC VIEW OF A NONLITERAL TRIBULATION PRECEDING THE SECOND COMING

The most important problem facing classic post-tribulationism is the necessity of explaining all prophetic events leading up to the second advent as either past or contemporaneous. The problems involved in such a viewpoint have led most contemporary posttribulationists away from the doctrine of imminency. By making the tribulation still future, posttribulationists allow a time period in which events predicted but not yet fulfilled can occur. The major problem of classic posttribulationism is to solve this problem of fulfillment of endtime prophecy.

For his position, Payne cites numerous Scriptures that support imminency and the concept of immediate expectation of the Lord's return. The Scriptures mentioned include many that relate generally to the second coming of Christ and others that speak specifically of the rapture. The presentation is confusing because verses are often included with little attention to their context or subject matter. Most expositors recognize that Scriptures relating to the rapture can be construed as presenting the event as imminent. It is also true that many passages relating to Christ's coming to set up His kingdom and to close the tribulation are presented as imminent for those living in the great tribulation. To put all these passages together, however, as proving that the second coming of Christ is imminent has not gained favor with most posttribulationists nor with those of other points of view.

While it is impossible to treat Payne's discussion thoroughly here, his extensive quotation of Scripture should be mentioned. Regarding "the time of the church's hope," he cites Isaiah 25:6-11; Matthew 24:29-31; Luke 17:24; Romans 8:18-21; 1 Corinthians 15:51,52; 1 Thessalonians 4:16,17; 2 Thessalonians 1:6-8; 2:1-2; Titus 2:12,13; Revelation 7:3,4; 14:3,4; 20:4,5.[17] He also discusses what he calls "contributory passages" and includes Isaiah 26:19-21; Daniel 12:1,2; Acts 1:11; Romans 11:15; 1 Corinthians 1:7; 1 Thessalonians 4:14-17; 5:2-6; 1 Timothy 6:14; 2 Timothy 4:8; 1 Peter 1:6,7,13; 5:4; Revelation 2:25,26; 14:14-16.

In support of imminency Payne mentions the following as "valid passages": Matthew 24:42–25:13; Luke 12:36-40; Romans 8:19,23,25; 1 Corinthians 1:7; Philippians 3:20; 4:5; 1 Thessalonians 1:9,10; Titus 2:12,13; James 5:7,8; Jude 21; and Revelation 16:15.[18]

The problem of how to solve predicted events which have not taken place and which are scheduled to occur before the second coming does not go away simply by quoting these many Scriptures. The problems surface immediately when certain questions are asked. A number of prophecies occur in Scripture such as Peter's predicted execution, the implication that a long time occurs between the first and second comings of Christ, and the prediction that Paul was to die. Prophecies of the destruction of Jerusalem also are presented as preceding the second advent. In an extended discussion of this kind of problem, Payne takes the position that while these were hindrances to imminency in the first century, they no longer existed as far as the early church fathers were concerned and certainly are no problem to us today. He also noted that it was not a practical problem for most of the early Christians, as they were not aware of these predictions.[19]

The more serious problems concern the prophetic program. One of these is the prophetic fulfillment of Daniel 9:27 predicting a final seven-year period and Daniel 12:9-12 in reference to the desecration of the temple. Payne solves this by applying it to the second century B.C. and holds that it is already fulfilled much in the style of many amillenarians.[20] However, because Christ predicted the abomination of desolation as a future event, making a second century B.C. fulfillment impossible, Payne refers this to the destruction of Jerusalem in A.D. 70. In a word, Payne spiritualizes these prophecies and does not expect literal fulfillment. His short dismissal of the possibility of future fulfillment is not convincing.

Even more pointed is the question of the rise of the Antichrist or a world ruler in the endtime. He states, "The question then arises, Is the Antichrist potentially present at this moment?"[21]

Payne goes on to point out how many identifications of the Antichrist have occurred in history that have proved false. The papacy at the time of the Protestant Reformation is no longer a live option and, as he states, "Hitler and Mussolini are now dead."[22] Payne in effect says that we need not ask this question, as surely someone at the time of Christ's return will qualify. He states, "The classic view of Christ's imminent return asks only that some such contemporary situation *could* be the setting for the end. Christ has promised that He will return sometime; and after all, an unusually apt candidate for the Antichrist is Nikita Khrushchev right today!"[23] Of course, Payne would himself no longer offer this candidate who seemed appropriate in 1962. In a word, Payne does not offer any real solution to this problem and does not face realistically the need for a detailed exegetical explanation. In effect he states the problem has a solution, but does not offer any in detail.

A further difficulty appears in Payne's interpretation of the Book of Revelation. In Appendix A, "An Analysis of the Book of Revelation," he attempts "a synthesis of the preterist, historical, and futurist systems of interpretation, employing each method at those points where it would seem best suited to the context concerned."[24] It takes little insight into the Book of Revelation to realize how completely subjective such an approach is. Payne has no consistent principle of interpretation and seizes any explanation that seems to avoid contradiction of his prophetic scheme. In effect Payne has to interpret the entire book in such a way that everything is fulfilled through chapter 18 in order to permit the second coming at any moment in chapter 19. The classic view of posttribulationism requires almost a completely nonliteral tribulation and a denial of any specific sequence of prophetic events preceding the second coming of Christ as being still future. Conservative interpreters of the Bible, whether posttribulational or pretribulational, have accordingly rejected Payne's point of view in support of his doctrine of imminency, and Payne stands virtually alone.

The Classic View of a Literal Millennium

A curious fact concerning current discussion of posttribulationism as opposed to pretribulationism is that it has been conducted almost entirely by premillenarians. Payne is not an exception, and in offering his classic view of posttribulationism he claims the support of the early church in his premillennial interpretation of the second advent of Christ. Although Payne assumes rather than attempts to prove his premillennialism, as it is not in the purpose of his discussion, he states in his analysis of Revelation 20–22, "Satan is bound and the resurrected Christian dead reign with Christ on earth 1,000 years" (20:1-6), and he goes on to speak of "Satan's final revolt and defeat. . . . The final judgment (20:10-15). The new heaven and earth: New Jerusalem" (21–22:5).[25]

From the standpoint of biblical interpretation, the fact that classic posttribulationism is also premillennial demonstrates its inherent inconsistency. The posttribulationism advanced by the classic interpretation depends almost completely on taking the tribulation in a nonliteral sense and in effect denies that there will be a literal tribulation period as such. If principles of interpretation permit the complete spiritualization of Revelation 1–18, on what logical grounds can chapters 19–22 suddenly be considered highly literal?

It is this very point that has caused some posttribulationists who were originally premillennial to embrace amillennialism. They argue that if the tribulation can be spiritualized to the extent that it is done by classic posttribulationism, then there is no adequate justification for interpreting the millennium itself literally. It is probably for this reason that most premillenarians today, even if they are posttribulational, reject the classic form of posttribulationism of the early church while at the same time embracing the premillennialism that characterized the church in the first two centuries.

SUMMARY

In summarizing classic posttribulationism as illustrated in the writings of J. Barton Payne, it has been demonstrated that four major propositions are involved: (1) Classic posttribulationism holds to the imminency of the second coming of Christ as an event that could occur any day; (2) It holds that the second coming is posttribulational, that is, coming after events that describe the time of trouble preceding the second advent; (3) In order to preserve the imminency of the second coming of Christ, it adopts a nonliteral interpretation of the tribulation, finding the events fulfilled either in the past or in the contemporary situation; (4) In spite of an almost total commitment to nonliteral interpretation of prophecies relating to the tribulation, the classic view holds with the early church fathers to a literal millennium following the second coming of Christ.

Most conservative expositors, regardless of their eschatological positions, reject classic posttribulationism because of its inherent inconsistency of combining in one system a very literal interpretation of the last four chapters of Revelation while at the same time holding to an almost completely nonliteral interpretation of the preceding chapters. The problems inherent in this position also explain why most adherents to a completely nonliteral interpretation of the earlier chapters of Revelation are amillennial rather than premillennial and apply the nonliteral interpretation to both the tribulation and the millenium. Although many posttribulationists would undoubtedly agree with some of the arguments advanced by Payne against pretribulationism, contemporary posttribulationism has largely abandoned premillennialism on the one hand in favor of amillennialism and has abandoned the doctrine of imminency in favor of a deferred second coming of Christ.

Probably the most evident fault of classic posttribulationism is its logical inconsistency. The early church fathers were obviously wrong in believing they were already in the great tribulation and other events of the last days. It was partly for this reason that they held to imminency. Payne wants to ignore this error in judgment of the early church fathers and accept their conclusions anyway. A conclusion is no stronger than its premises, and if the early fathers were wrong in their premises, they were also wrong in their conclusions. Most posttribulationists accordingly have abandoned the precise interpretation of the early fathers and the classic view of posttribulationism.

Notes

[1] Hal Lindsey et al., *When Is Jesus Coming Again?* (Carol Stream, Ill.: Creation House, 1974), p. 64.

[2] J. Barton Payne, *Encyclopedia of Biblical Prophecy* (New York: Harper & Row, 1973).

[3] J. Barton Payne, *The Imminent Appearing of Christ* (Grand Rapids: Wm. B. Eerdmans Publishing Co., 1962).

[4] George Ladd, *The Blessed Hope* (Grand Rapids: Wm. B. Eerdmans Publishing Co., 1956).

[5] John F. Walvoord, *The Rapture Question* (Findlay, Ohio: Dunham Publishing Co., 1957).

[6] Payne, *Imminent Appearing*, p. 161.

[7] Ibid., p. 85.

[8] Ibid., p. 86.

[9] Ibid.

[10] Ibid., p. 12.

[11] Ibid., pp. 15-16.

[12] Ibid., pp. 12-13.

[13] Ibid., p. 13.

[14] Ibid.

[15] Ibid., p. 17.

[16] Ibid., p. 21.

[17] Ibid., pp. 53-65.

[18] Ibid., pp. 95-102.

[19] Ibid., pp. 90-91.

[20] Ibid., pp. 116-20.

[21] Ibid., p. 121.

[22] Ibid.

[23] Ibid.

[24] Ibid., p. 170.

[25] Ibid., p. 176.

Chapter 3

Semiclassic Posttribulational Interpretation

If the eschatology of liberal scholarship is excluded, probably the majority view of posttribulationism can be classified as semiclassic. Because of the great diversity of viewpoints among the posttribulationists themselves, it is difficult to establish broad categories such as this in the study of posttribulationism today. However, in contrast to the purely classic view of J.Barton Payne, described in the previous chapter, and the purely futurist views of George E. Ladd and Robert H. Gundry, most contemporary posttribulationists can be designated as semiclassicists.

Within this broad category several subdivisions can be noted. First, some posttribulationists emphasize the contemporary character of the tribulation; while not insisting that all predicted events prior to the second coming have been fulfilled, they assert as their major point that the church is already in the great tribulation. Hence they argue it is folly to debate whether the church will be raptured before the tribulation. Second, some posttribulationists in this school of thought who are contending that the church is already in tribulation find certain aspects of the tribulation still future. These unfulfilled aspects may be limited to certain major events which are yet to be fulfilled or major persons who are yet to be revealed. They assume, in contrast to the classic position, that the second coming could not occur any day. Third, some like Alexander Reese find a specific seven-year period still future, as anticipated in Daniel 9:27, but tend to find some of the predictions of the Book of Revelation as contemporary or past and accordingly are not, strictly speaking, futurists like George E. Ladd. When posttribulationists charge pretribulationists with not always agreeing among themselves on some details, they do not seem to realize the extent of diversity of opinion in their own ranks, even when subdivided into broad categories. In the analysis of semiclassic posttribulationism which follows, the main trends will be traced even though there may be some variations from the broad trend.

THE SEMICLASSIC CLAIM TO BE
THE HISTORICAL INTERPRETATION

A major emphasis in most posttribulational presentations is the argument that they represent the historical view of the church and that pretribulationism arose only 150 years ago. Alexander Reese, for instance, referring to pretribulationism in his preface, says, "These views, which began to be propagated a little over one hundred years ago in the separatist movements of Edward Irving and J. N. Darby, have spread to the remotest corners of the earth, and enlisted supporters in most of the Reformed Churches in Christendom, including the Mission field."[1] The argument that posttribulationism must be accepted as true because it has been the view of the entire church until recently has been emphasized and reemphasized. Long lists of great scholars who are posttribulational are often compiled usually without regard as to whether they are premillennial, postmillennial, or amillennial, as if that made no difference. Also, there is almost complete disregard of the varieties of opinion among these posttribulationists in arguments which support their conclusion. Posttribulationists advancing this view take for granted that the posttribulationism of today, and especially their particular type of it, is precisely what the church has held through the centuries.

The fact is that contemporary semiclassic posttribulationism differs from the historical view in a number of particulars. Second-century premillenarians interpreted contemporary events as identifying their generation as being in the endtime. History has proved that they were wrong, and events that they identified as proof were not events of the endtime. The same error can be observed in identifying contemporary posttribulationism with that of the Protestant Reformers. Some of the Reformers identified contemporary events as being in the endtime and looked for the coming of the Lord either momentarily or soon. Again their posttribulationism was based on an error in judgment. Most contemporary posttribulationists are more cautious and concede that many years may elapse before the second coming will be fulfilled.

The element of imminency is usually lacking in the semiclassic posttribulational interpretation. While it is true that the postapostolic church did not understand or teach pretribulationism in the modern sense, neither did they teach posttribulationism as it is being advanced today. The fact is, the early church, concerned with many other problems, did not resolve the tension between believing that Christ could come at any moment and the fact that many prophetic events had to be fulfilled before He could come again. Most modern interpreters believe that the early church fathers were quite immature in many areas of doctrine, as witnessed by the long centuries which elapsed before such doctrines as the Trinity, sin, and justification were carefully formulated.

Because the early church, beginning with the third century, tended to abandon the literal interpretation of prophecy, their principles of interpretation did not permit any real advance in the understanding of the prophetic program. Each succeeding generation seems to have spiritualized prophecies to fit its own day, only to have history prove that they were wrong. The historical argument, while it is commonly advanced by posttribulationism, is therefore an insufficient basis to determine the issues between pretribulationism and posttribulationism. The issue, as most conservative theologians agree, is the question concerning what the Bible teaches. The very fact that posttribulationists differ so radically in their interpretation of major elements of prophecy related to the endtime should make clear to an impartial observer that they have not resolved their tensions and problems. As will be shown, the reason for this is their lack of agreement on principles of interpretation as well as their exegesis of key passages.

THE DOCTRINE OF THE TRIBULATION IN
SEMICLASSIC POSTTRIBULATIONISM

Posttribulationists are not in agreement on the character, nature, and extent of the time of trouble preceding the second coming of Christ. Though they hold that the church will go through the tribulation, they disagree among themselves as to what the tribulation is. In general, they fall into three groups: (1) those who hold that the tribulation extends throughout the entire age from the first coming of Christ to the second coming; (2) those who hold that the church is already in tribulation but that the great tribulation is still future; (3) the futuristic school which, in contrast to the semiclassic interpretation, holds that the tribulation is completely future, usually identifying it as the last seven years preceding the second coming of Christ, based on a futuristic interpretation of Daniel 9:27 and Revelation 4–18.

In holding that the church must go through the tribulation, most posttribulationists tend to identify the church with Israel or at least hold that the church and Israel are both members of the spiritual community. As even pretribulationists agree that there are saved people in the tribulation time, posttribulationists assume that they have proved that the church itself is in this period. A familiar text used by posttribulationists is Matthew 24:31 NASB: "And He shall send forth His angels with a great sound of a trumpet, and they shall gather together His elect from the four winds, from one end of heaven to the other."

The term *elect* is commonly taken as referring to the church, and therefore because there are elect in the tribulation as proved by Matthew 24:31, they hold that the church is in the tribulation. Norman S. MacPherson, for instance, says, "There is nothing here to indicate who the *elect* are, although there is every likelihood that the term refers to the Church. . . ."[2] Alexander Reese goes a step further and says it is "supreme rubbish" to argue whether the *elect* is equivalent to the church.[3] Reese, of course, begs the whole question in assuming what he is trying to prove. Everyone agrees that the saved of all ages are the elect. The question is whether the term *church* and particular expressions like *the body of Christ* include all the elect. In the passage cited, some take the word *elect* to refer to Israel as an elect nation.

All agree that there are elect individuals in the great tribulation, but posttribulationists tend to assume without proof that this is identical in meaning to the church. While the word *church* is used to indicate a congregation or a physical assembly of people in both the Old and New Testaments, there is not a single instance in the entire Bible where the word *church*, as indicating a body of saints, is ever used in a passage dealing with the tribulation. It is this crucial point that posttribulationists fail to take into account. There will be a gathering of the elect at the end of the tribulation, but Matthew does not indicate anything concerning its nature and the purpose of the gathering as it relates to the introduction of the millennial kingdom. The strong, dogmatic statements of posttribulationism do not change the fact that Matthew mentions neither rapture nor resurrection in this passage.

The greatest confusion of posttribulationists, however, is in their concept of the tribulation itself. George L. Rose holds that the great tribulation began with the apostolic period. He states, "The record left us in the book of The Acts of the Apostles leaves no room to doubt that 'tribulation' began almost as soon as the church was born. . . ."[4] Rose goes on to point out that in Acts 8:1-3 there was "great persecution" of the church, and he holds that "great persecution" is the same as "great tribulation" and that the same word for tribulation is used in Matthew 24:21 in speaking of the "great tribulation." According to Rose, the church of course goes through the great tribulation because it is already in the great tribulation.

Fromow, in a similar way, holds that the church is already in the great tribulation. "The Church is *already* passing through 'the Great Tribulation.' "[5] Fromow goes on to say:

> This term *Great* embraces the whole period of the Church's course on earth and should not be confined to the final three and one-half years or the second half of Daniel's seventieth week of intensive tribulation. It began with the first saints after the Fall, includes all who washed their robes and made them white in the blood of the Lamb until the Second Advent of Christ.[6]

Fromow begins the great tribulation with Adam instead of with the early church. In holding this position, he ignores the plain teaching of Scripture that the great tribulation is the last three and one-half years preceding the second coming of Christ, as brought out in Daniel 12, where it is defined as a period of about 1,290 days and as it is defined in the Book of Revelation as a time of forty-two months (Rev. 13:5). This is why Christ used the great tribulation as the specific sign indicating that the second coming of Christ was near (Matt. 24:15-22).

The problem here, as it frequently is in posttribulational interpretation, is that the argument is based on a nonliteral interpretation of prophecy in which expressions like "the great tribulation" are spiritualized. All agree that the saints have had problems and tribulation since the beginning of the human race. The Bible teaches, however, that these present trials are not to be confused with the great tribulation, which is declared to be unprecedented and therefore unique, which will end the age preceding the second coming (Dan. 12:1; Matt. 24:21).

In contrast to the position that the church is already in the great tribulation, Alexander Reese definitely advances the concept that the seven-year period predicted by Daniel 9:27 as preceding the second advent is still future. In an extended discussion, he supports a literal view of this last seven-year period as being yet future. He states, "The eschatological character of the Seventieth Week is assumed throughout this volume...."[7] On the basis of his strong stand for a future period, Reese could be classified as a futurist like Ladd. However, in his treatment of the Book of Revelation dealing with the endtime trouble, Reese tends to support at least some of the findings of the historical school (which believes that the fulfillment of the seals is in some sense already under way), although he does not accept what he refers to as "the extravagances of the Historical School...."[8] Pretribulationists, of course, would agree with Reese that the last seven years preceding the second coming are still future.

Reese is in error, however, in holding that the futuristic view of the last seven years was held by the early church fathers. As Payne has brought out, the early fathers thought they were already in the period, and that is why they did not give consideration to a possible pretribulational interpretation. They tended to identify their persecutions with the persecution of the great tribulation. Like the early fathers, Martin Luther also held that the church was already in the great tribulation. Luther wrote, "The last day is at hand. My calendar has run out. I know nothing more in the Scriptures."[9] This diversity of opinion among the semiclassic posttribulationists should make clear that posttribulationism, as it is held by this school of thought, is not the same as that held by the early fathers; their constant assertion that they are in the tradition of the time-honored interpretation is only partially true.

Reese's viewpoint, of course, also pinpoints the crucial question as to whether the rapture of the church is imminent. Rose and Fromow (with Martin Luther) held that because we are already in the great tribulation, the rapture could occur any day. And at least some of the early fathers believed this also. But Reese, believing that the tribulation is yet future, cannot hold to the imminent rapture. In fact, he leaves without explanation why the rapture is uniformly presented as an imminent event in the New Testament.

The semiclassic view does not resolve the major problems which posttribulationism faces in interpreting the New Testament. It is evident by the various views of the tribulation itself that posttribulationists are almost in complete confusion as to what they mean by the church going through the great tribulation. It is also evident that they use differing methods of interpretation, some of them almost completely spiritualizing the tribulation and others, like Reese, taking it more literally.

While they argue against the idea that the Bible does not place the church in this time of great tribulation, their arguments always fall short of proof and frequently are circular in that they assume what they are trying to prove.

The basic problem of posttribulationists is that they have not agreed among themselves whether to interpret prophecy literally. The great majority do not use the literal method when it would teach a pretribulational rapture. They also differ among themselves on the important question of whether prophecy should be interpreted as teaching a future, literal millennium. Again and again, in examining posttribulational arguments, one is struck by their lack of uniformity in interpreting prophecy in a literal sense.

The fact remains, when all the evidence is sifted, that posttribulationists have yet to prove that the body of Christ is mentioned in any passage dealing with the great tribulation itself or the entire seven-year period leading up to the second coming. In view of the detailed prophecies that deal with this period — with Revelation 4–18 presenting a graphic picture of this endtime stage — it is most strange that there should be no mention of saints who can be identified as belonging to the church. This is especially odd in view of the fact that Revelation 2–3 deals specifically with the seven churches of Asia.

SEQUENCE OF EVENTS RELATED TO THE SECOND ADVENT

Another major problem of posttribulationism is that in the sequence of events relating to the second coming, there is no proof of a rapture of living saints or a resurrection of the church, the body of Christ. In the key passages on the second coming — such as Matthew 24, Jude, and Revelation 19 — there is no mention of either event. It is most impressive that when resurrection is mentioned in Revelation 20:4, it is specifically limited to the tribulation saints as contrasted to the church. If the tribulation saints were a part of the church, why was not the expression "the dead in Christ" used as in 1 Thessalonians 4? The fact that this group is singled out for resurrection, as if they were a special body of saints, points to the conclusion that the church had been previously raptured.

Posttribulationists also have never resolved the pressing question as to why there is a rapture at the second coming. If, as a matter of fact, the purpose of Christ is to establish His saints in the millennial kingdom, why would saints meet Christ in the air at the rapture if they are going to return immediately to the earth as the posttribulationists teach? Why would it not be preferable for the church to go into the millennium in their natural bodies as the Scriptures make clear other saints will do? The omission of any reference to rapture of living saints or to the resurrection of the church as the body of Christ specifically in the events related to the second coming of Christ to the earth is an argument from silence, but an impressive one. How strange that such an important doctrine should be omitted from Scriptures that are obviously detailing the major events of the second advent. Though the Old Testament saints are especially mentioned in Daniel 12:2 and the tribulation saints are mentioned in Revelation 20:4, the church, the body of Christ, is not included in these resurrections. Further, there is no evidence that *any* saints then living on earth will be translated at the time Christ comes back to set up His kingdom. It is clear to premillenarians at least that saints on earth at that time will enter the millennium in their natural bodies and populate the millennial earth.

In semiclassic posttribulationism, the chronic problems of this approach to eschatology emerge. The inconsistent use of the literal interpretation of prophecy characterizes all the proponents of semiclassic posttribulationism. While they take some prophecies literally, they tend to spiritualize any prophecy that would contradict posttribulationism. The improper use of the inductive method is also evident as they select in each passage what supports their view and ignore the facts that contradict it. In eschatology, as in all branches of theology, consistent use of principles of interpretation and proper consideration of all the facts bearing on the doctrine are absolutely essential. Semiclassic posttribulationism fails in these important areas.

Many exegetical problems face the posttribulationists in their attempts to establish biblical proofs for their conclusions. These will be discussed more at length in the examination of the overall presentation of posttribulationists. Next, however, the particular view of the futurist school and the new posttribulational dispensational interpretation of Robert H. Gundry need to be examined as major contributions to recent thought.

Notes

[1] Alexander Reese, *The Approaching Advent of Christ* (London: Marshall, Morgan & Scott, 1937), p. xi.

[2] Norman S. MacPherson, *Triumph through Tribulation* (Otego, N.Y.: First Baptist Church, 1944), p. 8.

[3] Reese, *The Approaching Advent of Christ*, p. 207.

[4] George L. Rose, *Tribulation till Translation* (Glendale, Calif.: Rose Publishing Co., 1942), p. 68.

[5] George H. Fromow, *Will the Church Pass through the Tribulation?* (London: Sovereign Grace Advent Testimony, n.d.), p. 2.

[6] Ibid.

[7] Reese, *Approaching Advent*, p. 30.

[8] Ibid., p. 33.

[9] Theodore G. Tappert, ed., *Luther's Words*, 56 vols. (Philadelphia: Fortress Press, 1967), 54:134.

Chapter 4

Futurist Posttribulational Interpretation

With the emergence of premillennialism in the nineteenth and twentieth centuries, a relatively new view of posttribulationism was advanced that can be called futurist. In contrast to the posttribulationism that characterized amillennialism and the Protestant Reformers, who considered themselves already in the tribulation, the new view contended that the last seven years of Daniel's prophecy of Israel's program revealed in Daniel 9:24-27 should be considered still future. In harmony with this position, it was often also contended that Revelation 4–18 describes a future rather than an historic situation. The leading twentieth-century exponent of the futurist view is George E. Ladd, who sets forth his position in his work *The Blessed Hope,* published in 1956.

THE PREMISES OF FUTURIST POSTTRIBULATIONISM

As illustrated in Ladd, futurist posttribulationism is built on the premise of premillenialism. He states, "One thing should be emphasized: the author would affirm his belief in the personal, premillennial second advent of Jesus Christ. He is looking for His coming; it is his Blessed Hope."[1]

In adopting premillennialism, Ladd also holds in all major respects a futurist view of the Book of Revelation. In general he follows the concept that there is yet ahead a seven-year period climaxing in a great tribulation that will fulfill literally the relevant prophecies of the Old and New Testaments. Ladd assumes the authority and accuracy of prophecy and usually interprets it literally, with some notable exceptions. The premises of Ladd's position accordingly require him to turn away from historic amillennialism as held by Augustine and the Protestant Reformers. Ladd offers a relatively new view of posttribulationism that differs in major respects from that held by the early fathers and Reformed theology. His major point of agreement with them, however, is that he places the rapture as occurring at the second coming of Christ after the time of tribulation.

In rejecting pretribulationism, Ladd also rejects dispensational interpretation. He distinguishes Israel from the church in some passages; in others he rejects a distinction, holding that promises given to Israel in the Old Testament should be interpreted as having a dual fulfillment, that is, fulfilled both in the church and in Israel. Ladd recognizes that dispensationalism naturally leads to pretribulationism, and therefore he devotes a chapter to a refutation of dispensationalism.

His arguments for posttribulationism are generally well presented in a persuasive way, and he attempts to avoid any unfair or discourteous treatment of those with whom he disagrees. His approach is that pretribulationism is a new doctrine not advanced until the early nineteenth century, in contrast to posttribulationism which is the traditional and historic position of the church.

THE HISTORICAL ARGUMENT FOR POSTTRIBULATIONISM

As pointed out in an earlier review of Ladd's *The Blessed Hope*,[2] the first third of his book is devoted to the historical argument for posttribulationism, although the work is introduced as "A Biblical Study of The Second Advent and The Rapture." Ladd himself says, "Let it be at once emphasized that we are not turning to the church fathers to find authority for either pre- or posttribulationism. The one authority is the Word of God, and we are not confined in the strait-jacket of tradition."[3]

In presenting the historical argument as it appears in most

posttribulational studies, Ladd attempts to prove that the post-tribulational return of Christ was the historic hope of the church from the beginning. In the second chapter of his work, "The Rise and Spread of Pretribulationism," he traces pretribulationism to the Plymouth Brethren movement in the early nineteenth century. His argument is designed to prove, first, that pretribulationism was unknown until the nineteenth century; second, that honored men of God have been posttribulationists; third, that pretribulationism started as a heresy and not through sound biblical studies. He quotes from eight of the early church fathers to the point that pretribulationism as it is taught today was unknown in the early church and contends that it never appeared until it was given in a special revelation to an erratic individual, Edward Irving, about 1830. Ladd claims that it was immediately accepted by Darby and his associates and widely proclaimed.

The statement of Ladd that pretribulationism was unknown until the nineteenth century is a half-truth. Pretribulationism as it is known today is comparatively recent, but the concept of imminency of the Lord's return — which is the important point — clearly dates to the early church.

It may be conceded, as Ladd points out, that some post-tribulationists have been honored expositors of the Word. The allegation of Ladd and others that pretribulationism started as a heresy, however, is a charge unworthy of a careful scholar. There is no more evidence for this than there is that Ladd's view started as a heresy, even though it is comparatively new.

This charge usually is associated with the idea that Darby received the doctrine of pretribulationism from Edward Irving, a pre-Pentecostalist of doubtful orthodoxy, and Margaret Mac-Donald, who had a vision under demonic influence. This charge has been built up by Dave MacPherson in his book *The Incredible Cover-Up*, labeled as "The True Story on the Pre-Trib Rapture."[4] MacPherson is a newsman and has combined in this new publication two previously published books, *The Unbelievable Pre-Trib Origin* and *The Late Great Pre-Trib Rapture*, which in turn were preceded by numerous mimeographed polemics against pretribulationism.

Significantly MacPherson made these charges against pretribulationism and then afterward went to great lengths to find historic verification. To his credit, he has brought to light what contributions Irving and MacDonald made on this subject. Readers will be impressed that as a newsman MacPherson builds a strong case for his position, but will be less impressed when they begin to analyze what he has actually proved.

At least five criticisms can be made of MacPherson's argument.

First, there was no "cover-up." To charge pretribulationist scholars with a plot to cover up the origin of the pretribulational position is to impugn their integrity. The fact is, most pretribulationists derived their views from biblical exegesis rather than from the history of the doctrine. The question, after all, is what the Bible teaches. If it were true — which it does not seem to be — that MacDonald and Irving were the first to arrive at the pretribulational doctrine, it still would not prove that pretribulationism was wrong. To charge pretribulationism, however, with a cover-up is a slander.

Second, it is most significant that all the information MacPherson offers comes from ardent posttribulationists — as illustrated in referring to the statement of Samuel P. Tregelles that the pretribulational rapture view originated in the year 1832 in Edward Irving's church. There is evidence that the statement of Tregelles was a false story first told by Tregelles in 1864, more than thirty years after the supposed incident. R. A. Huebner, carefully analyzing the various documents coming from Irving and MacDonald, demonstrates by long quotations that nine years before 1864 Tregelles had attributed it to Judaizers in an attempt to defame pretribulationism and at that time apparently had not heard the idea that Irving had originated a secret rapture.[5] Tregelles' charge in 1855 that pretribulationism came from Judaizers is just as unsupported an allegation as his statement of 1864.

What can be said about Tregelles as a prejudiced witness is true of all the other witnesses MacPherson quotes, who are our sole source of information on Irving and MacDonald.

Third, the evidence offered by MacPherson fails to support his allegation that either Margaret MacDonald or Edward Irving were clearly pretribulationists. While we are indebted to Mac-

Pherson for his research on the subject, it is significant that he made the charges long before he did the research, and it may be that his discoveries contradict rather than support his conclusions. Huebner makes the startling statement in regard to MacPherson's supposed discovery of the origin of pretribulationism that the evidence, instead of proving MacPherson right, rather proves him wrong. Huebner comments, "It thus happens, under the good hand of God, that He has ordered it that a posttribulationist has rediscovered the refutation of this slander, insofar as it has to do with Scotland, Miss M. M. and 1830."[6]

Readers of MacPherson's *Incredible Cover-Up* will undoubtedly be impressed by the many long quotations, most of which are only window dressing for what he is trying to prove. When it gets down to the point of proving that either MacDonald or Irving was pretribulationist, the evidence gets very muddy. The quotations MacPherson cites do not support his conclusion. In brief, MacPherson proves that MacDonald and Irving were not traditional posttribulationists, but he does not prove that they were pretribulationists.

MacPherson quotes at length an account of the incident in which Margaret was supposed to have received the gift of prophecy. As written up by the ardent posttribulationist Norton, Margaret MacDonald is reputed to have heard the trump of God and heavenly hosts singing and then had a vision of the Lord's coming.[7] Norton also records a second experience and quotes one of Margaret's sisters, who describes her experience which included her own healing and the outpouring of the Holy Spirit on her brother James. In the quotations from MacPherson, one searches in vain for any clear pretribulational teaching.

It would not be difficult to quote numerous posttribulational writers who state that Irving and MacDonald were pretribulationists — including Ladd, Reese, Gundry, and Payne. Others are content to start with Darby. When a search is made for proof that Irving and MacDonald were pretribulationists, one discovers something amazing: the proof is lacking, even in the extensive quotations by Dave MacPherson. Huebner has proved conclusively by a series of quotations that Irving actually believed the church was already at the stage of the seventh seal, the seventh trumpet, and the seventh vial of the Book of Revelation, a point in time that posttribulationists place at the end of the tribulation. In December 1831, *The Morning Watch*, published by Irving, stated the following: "that the seventh seal has been opened, the seventh trumpet sounded, the seventh vial commenced: but it is only to this last-mentioned portion of prophecy that we shall at present direct our attention. We have, blessed be God, lived to see the commencement of the seventh vial, DURING THE OUT-POURING OF WHICH THE LORD WILL COME!"[8]

How can any interpret this as a pretribulational rapture? This was published more than a year *after* the supposed revelation in 1830.

While the exact order of events as held by the Irvingites is confused to say the least, there is little here to correspond to the normal teaching of pretribulationism. It is also clear that as the Irvingites itemized certain prophecies still to be fulfilled before the rapture, they did not hold the "any moment" doctrine of the rapture — and no one has been able to quote Irving as holding this position. The entire argument in support of Irving as a pre-tribulationist is shattered by the thorough documentation of Huebner.[9] MacPherson in his entire work nowhere proves that Irving was a pretribulationist.

What then can be said about Margaret MacDonald?

Most of the quotations by MacPherson are from people other than Margaret MacDonald herself, and are second- or third-hand accounts. Many were published for the first time many years after the event: they would not stand in any court of law. An examination of these quotations, moreover, leaves the reader amazed: after searching diligently, one finds no clear statement that Mac-Donald held to a pretribulation rapture. She did apparently distinguish more than one return of Christ and, in fact, has some similarity to the partial-rapture view. But it is not at all clear that any of the raptures mentioned would occur *before* the tribulation begins; rather they were a series of events at the climax of the great tribulation. This does not prevent MacPherson's claiming that Margaret MacDonald clearly states the pretribulational view.

MacPherson quotes a letter written by Francis Sitwell to his sister Mary dealing with the influence of Margaret's "pre-trib views" upon others.[10] A careful reading of the letter, however, does not reveal pretribulational views at all. The nearest statement that could be construed to be the pretribulational view is when Francis Sitwell says, "It is because there is no safety where you are, because you cannot be sealed where you are, it is because you are not sealed you must be left in the tribulations, while those who obeyed His voice shall be caught up to meet Him."[11] The deliverance from the tribulation here cited seems to be a deliverance from the last portion of the tribulation rather than all of it. One wonders how MacPherson can be so blatant in his claim of presenting "The True Story of the Pre-Trib Rapture" when, as a matter of fact, the quotations he cites give no solid basis for this.

While MacDonald's and Irving's views do not correspond to some of the posttribulational interpretations today, neither do they correspond to any clear pretribulational view such as Darby later expounded. It is amazing that so many well-known scholars make broad statements about this matter when the proof is lacking, even in all the documentation that Dave MacPherson offers. To have the matter still obscure and unproved despite the abundant citations offered indicates that the conclusion that MacDonald and Irving were pretribulationists is simply unsupported.

The distinction between the *parousia* and the *epiphany* attributed to MacDonald does not prove the point because both are, for all practical purposes, posttribulational rather than pretribulational comings. As Huebner sums it up, "It is nigh incredible to think that anyone could attempt to derive dispensational truth or the pretribulation rapture out of a post-tribulational, invisible epiphany to be followed shortly after by a parousia!"[12]

Thus a search of available material indicates that the Irvingites did not hold to a pretribulational rapture or to an imminent rapture. In fact, they claimed that a number of prophecies had to be fulfilled first. Therefore it should be concluded that "The Incredible Cover-Up" of Dave MacPherson is no cover-up at all because there is nothing to cover up. The supposed pretribulationism of MacDonald and Irving is so elusive that even MacPherson cannot prove his point.

Fourth, if for the sake of argument it were admitted that Irving and MacDonald held the pretribulational position, there is still absolutely no documentary proof that Darby derived his views from them. MacPherson's claim that Darby must have known because he knew other facts about the Irvingites is nullified because Darby would also have known that Irving was not a pretribulationist. Both the source and the link of this supposed transmission of pretribulationism to Darby are lacking.

Fifth, any careful student of Darby soon discovers that he did not get his eschatological views from men, but rather from his doctrine of the church as the body of Christ, a concept no one claims was revealed supernaturally to Irving or MacDonald. Darby's views undoubtedly were gradually formed, but they were theologically and biblically based rather than derived from Irving's pre-Pentecostal group.

The whole controversy as aroused by Dave MacPherson's claims has so little supporting evidence, despite his careful research, that one wonders how he can write his book with a straight face. Pretribulationists should be indebted to Dave MacPherson for exposing the facts, namely, that there is no proof that MacDonald or Irving originated the pretribulation rapture teaching.

Two additional major faults, however, occur in Ladd's presentation. First, he does not seem to realize that his view of posttribulationism is quite different from that of the early church and is, in fact, of more recent origin than pretribulationism. Second, he denies the imminence of the Lord's return, that is, that the Lord could come at any time. This contrasts with the imminence held by the early fathers and revived by the Protestant Reformers. Many posttribulationists, such as J. Barton Payne, concede that the early fathers believed in imminency and that this is the historic position.[13]

The argument that the church fathers' being posttribulational makes this the correct interpretation is faulty. If Ladd is correct that pretribulationism as it is taught today is not found in the early fathers, neither is Ladd's brand of posttribulationism. The early fathers were not clear on many details of their eschatology, and many did not write at all on this subject. Where they did, it seems that in the first two centuries they were definitely premillennial rather than amillennial. Not until the Reformation were the authority of Scripture and the imminency of Christ's return once again firmly recognized. And not until premillennialism became a major issue in the last century could pretribulationism even be considered.

The often-repeated charge that Darby secured his pretribulationism from Edward Irving has never been actually documented. One can hardly account for the wide acceptance of pretribulationism by Plymouth Brethren, who were devoted students of the Bible, to the offering of this view by a person who had no reputation for orthodoxy. A more cogent explanation is that pretribulationism arose as a refinement of premillennialism based on literal interpretation of prophecy which made it difficult to harmonize the doctrine of the rapture with the second coming of Christ to set up His kingdom. Most pretribulationists obviously base their views on the Bible, not on the historic background of the doctrine.

In his historical analysis, Ladd correctly points out that pretribulationism was not the unanimous position of premillennialism in the nineteenth century. Much of his chapter on the history recounts those who abandoned pretribulationism for posttribulationism, with the implication that the former does not stand up to careful study. However, what this proves is that the pretribulationists did not know why they were pretribulationists. The argument that there was a broad trend away from pretribulationism is refuted by Ladd's own admission that pretribulationism has wide acceptance and current vitality as a doctrine. Undoubtedly there are conversions both ways. If pretribulationism was not known until 1830, certainly there must be some biblical basis for its widespread acceptance at the present time.

On the basis of his documentation, Ladd concludes that the early church was posttribulational, that pretribulationism arose in the nineteenth century, and that some who accepted pretribulationism later departed from it. His conclusion that, therefore, pretribulationism is unscriptural remains the question.

The Argument From Vocabulary of the Blessed Hope

In chapter 3 of his presentation, Ladd takes the position that the three Greek words for the rapture — *coming* or *presence*

(parousia), *appearing (epiphaneia)*, and *revelation (apokalypsis)* —
are technical words that must refer only to one event, that is, the
second coming after the tribulation. This is a broad assumption,
faulty in hermeneutics as well as in exegesis, and is an error
sometimes held also by pretribulationists. The basic rule for the
interpretation of any word in the Bible must be its context. Obviously words like *coming, appearing,* and *revelation* are not in themselves technical words, and if they are used in a technical sense in
the Bible it must be sustained by an examination of every reference.

Some pretribulationists have attempted to identify some of
these terms with the rapture and others with the second coming.
Most expositors, whether pretribulational or posttribulational,
however, hold that they are not technical words in themselves and
must be interpreted by their context. If the first coming and the
second coming of Christ were both referred to as "comings," it
would not prove that the two comings were the same coming.
Likewise, using the same terms for the rapture and the second
coming does not make them the same event. These words are
general words, and Ladd's entire chapter 3 begs the question, that
is, it assumes what he is trying to prove. If the Scriptures were
attempting to present a pretribulation rapture, how else could
they do it without using the same words?

The argument on terminology is continued in his chapter 4
on the subject "The Tribulation, the Rapture, and the Resurrection." The argument here turns on the lack of reference to the
rapture in important passages dealing with the second coming of
Christ. He discusses Matthew 24:4-14; 2 Thessalonians 2; and
Revelation 8:16. He concludes:

> Our survey of these three great passages which set forth the coming
> of Antichrist and the Great Tribulation shows clearly that none of
> them asserts that the Church is to be raptured at the beginning of
> the Tribulation. When such a doctrine is attributed to these Scrip-
> tures, it is an inference and not the assertion of the Word of God.[14]

Such an argument is obviously based on an illogical premise. Two
of the three passages are admittedly dealing with the second
coming of Christ after the tribulation. The fact is that they do not
talk about the rapture at all because no rapture occurs in connec-

tion with it. Second Thessalonians 2 deals with the rapture in verse 1 and with the second coming in verse 8, but this does not make them the same event. The problem is Ladd's, not that of the pretribulationist. The silence about the rapture in two of the passages points to the conclusion that the rapture does not occur at the second coming.

None of the passages dealing with Christ's coming after the tribulation ever includes a reference to the translation of living saints. Even Ladd, while not referring to it in this chapter, later admits, "nor does the Word of God explicitly place the Rapture at the end of the Tribulation."[15] He nevertheless contends, "If a pretribulation rapture is a Biblical doctrine, it ought to be clearly set forth in the Scriptures which prophesy the Rapture of the Church."[16] Ladd does not seem to realize that the same argument holds against the posttribulational point of view. Why is not a posttribulation rapture "clearly set forth in the Scriptures which prophesy the Rapture of the Church"? If pretribulational doctrine is based on an inference, so is posttribulationism.

It is noteworthy that in his entire discussion, Ladd practically ignores the three principal Scriptures revealing the rapture — John 14:3; 1 Corinthians 15:51,52; and 1 Thessalonians 4:13-18. If Ladd is going to deal with the biblical content of the rapture, why does he ignore the principal passages? The answer is, of course, that there is no explicit teaching of posttribulationism in these passages and it does not advance his argument.

In discussing the word *resurrection*, Ladd refers specifically to Revelation 20:4, where there is a resurrection that is obviously posttribulational. Ladd here begs the question and rejects categorically the concept that there can be any other resurrection before the first resurrection. He argues, therefore, that the rapture must occur at the second coming.

The idea that the first resurrection can be in more than one stage is taught in 1 Corinthians 15:23,24. Three stages (*tagma*) of the resurrection of the saints are included: Christ, first; those at His coming, second; and those at the end, third. While the third resurrection can be debated (as it is not clear whether it refers to a resurrection of the saints at the end of the millennium or refers to the resurrection of the wicked), this passage clearly distinguishes the resurrection of Christ from the resurrection of the saints and declares that they are stages. To this could be added Matthew 27:52,53, which speaks of a token resurrection of saints immediately after the resurrection of Christ. The resurrection at the rapture and the resurrection of the tribulation saints in Revelation 20:4 are not the "first" in the sense that no resurrection occurred before; they are first only in the sense that they occur first or before the final resurrection, which is the resurrection of the wicked at the end of the millennium. Actually the order of resurrections is Christ first, then the resurrection of Matthew 27, then the resurrection of the rapture, and then the resurrection of the tribulation dead. To this should be added the resurrection of Old Testament saints, which even pretribulationists place at the end of the tribulation. In other words, Ladd is once again assuming what he is trying to prove, namely, that the rapture and its attendant resurrection occur at the same time as the resurrection of the tribulation saints. He overlooks that in Revelation 20:4 the specific resurrection refers only to tribulation saints, not to anyone else. Ladd is inferring that the rapture occurs after the tribulation, but has not proved it.

A fact uniformly ignored by all posttribulationists in their exposition of Revelation 20:4 is that the resurrection here clearly comes *after* Christ has come to earth. In the preceding context, Christ returns to earth in chapter 19, destroys His enemies, and in chapter 20 binds Satan. Judgment seats are then set up on the earth. In connection with judgment, the resurrection of the tribulation saints takes place after Christ has come to earth. In the posttribulational order of events, the resurrection should have taken place while Christ was coming from heaven to earth according to 1 Thessalonians 4:13-18, before the events which follow His second coming. Accordingly a resurrection in the process of Christ's coming to earth becomes highly questionable and poses a serious problem to posttribulationists. It confirms the pretribulational contention that there is no rapture or resurrection while He is descending from heaven to the earth at His second coming.

Is Posttribulationism a Valid Inference?

In his chapter 5 Ladd faces the problem that posttribulationism is an inference. He approaches it, however, from the question as to whether pretribulationism is a valid inference. The fact that a whole chapter is devoted to this is most significant, as it is an admission that this is a vulnerable point in the posttribulational argument. While it is not possible to deal with all of his presentation, the salient points can be discussed.

Ladd concedes at the outset: "We will admit that even if Scripture did not explicitly affirm a pretribulation rapture, it is possible that the totality of scriptural data would demand such a conclusion; and in this case, it would be a valid inference."[17] In the discussion that follows, he offers a comprehensive refutation of arguments commonly used by pretribulationism. In other words, his method is to attack pretribulationism rather than to support posttribulationism.

The important question of the usage of the word *church* is handled only briefly, although it is a major consideration. He admits that the word *church* is not found in any tribulation passage, but replies that the word is never used in the Book of Revelation "to designate the Church in its totality."[18] This, however, is not the real point. The burden of proof is on the posttribulationist to prove that the church is in the tribulation. If even a local church could be found in the period, it would be a point in favor of posttribulationism. Ladd, however, like most posttribulationists passes over this point hurriedly because actually posttribulationism has no answer to this difficulty in its system. When it comes right down to it, its adherents lack any positive proof that the church—the *ekklesia*—is ever found in the tribulation period or, for that matter, is indicated in the sequence of events related to the second coming to set up Christ's kingdom. As this is a key doctrine of pretribulationism, his rather weak and inadequate treatment of this problem is a defect in his argument. In contrast he devotes pages to indecisive questions.

Dealing with the question as to whether pretribulationism is a valid inference, Ladd finds it appropriate to ignore one of the most important pretribulation arguments for the necessity of an interval.[19] Pretribulationists have often pointed out that if every living saint is raptured at the time of the second coming this would, in itself, separate all saints from unsaved people and would leave none to populate the millennial earth. Ladd does not deal with this problem at all. Some of his fellow posttribulationists — such as Rose in his book *Tribulation till Translation* and Gundry in his recent work *The Rapture and the Tribulation* — do face this problem. Both postulate a second chance for those not saved at the time of the second coming. According to them, there is a time period between the rapture and the beginning of the millennium during which people can still come to Christ. Rose puts this in a forty-day period between the rapture and the judgment of the nations in Matthew 25.

The only posttribulational answer to the problem facing premillenarians in regard to populating the millennial earth is to give a second chance to those not saved and therefore not raptured at the rapture. However, the Scriptures do not reveal such a second chance. Ladd's silence on the whole matter seems to indicate he does not have a solution to this major problem of posttribulationism.

In discussing the concept that both views of the tribulation are based on inference, posttribulationists ignore that this is a much greater problem for them than for the pretribulationists. If the rapture of the church is imminent — as it is consistently presented in the rapture passages — there is no need to itemize the events that precede or follow. On the other hand, posttribulationists are faced with the fact that numerous Scriptures itemize in detail the events leading up to the second coming of Christ and the event itself when He comes to the earth to bring in His millennial kingdom. The silence of any mention of a translation of the church or of a resurrection in the process of coming from heaven to earth is, under these circumstances, a very eloquent silence. If Revelation 4–18 provides a comprehensive revelation of the steps leading up to the second coming in chapter 19, and if this is the major point of this entire book, for the rapture to be left only to an inference is very difficult to explain. Posttribulationists do not answer satisfactorily this important and weighty objection to their interpretation.

THE ARGUMENT FROM COMMANDS TO "WATCH"

In supporting his futurist view of posttribulationism, Ladd

devotes considerable attention to various Greek words used in the New Testament to indicate the attitude of watchfulness. His point is to prove that the idea of the imminency of the Lord's return is not involved. Here his fallacy is that he attempts to make a general word a technical word, much as Reese and others have done. This violates the basic rule of interpretation that a word must be considered in its context. In some cases, the context is clearly in reference to the second coming of Christ to establish His kingdom. In other cases, it is in connection with the rapture.

The important point is that each of the various exhortations to watch for the Lord's coming has its own context. Sometimes the context has to do with the return after the tribulation and obviously refers to people living at that time. The context in such instances makes clear, as in Matthew 24–25, that watching for the Lord's return has special pertinence *after* the signs appear, but not before. By contrast, however, where the rapture is clearly in view, no signs are given but the believers are exhorted to look for the Lord's return itself (cf. John 14:3; 1 Cor. 15:51,52; 1 Thess. 4:13-18). It may be conceded that some pretribulationists have overdone the argument based on these exhortations, but the similarity of expressions for expectancy of the rapture and the Lord's return after the tribulation does not prove that the two events are one and the same. Both are events to be expected, even if the expectancy may differ according to the context.

Wrath or Tribulation?

In a separate chapter, Ladd deals with the question as to whether divine wrath and tribulation are one and the same, and he rightly concludes that the church cannot experience divine wrath although it may experience tribulation. Most pretribulationists will concede this point. Ladd's argument, however, passes over the main point in the distinction as it is commonly presented by pretribulationists; the real issue is avoided rather than faced.

The point is not that the church will escape the wrath of God, but that it will escape the *time* of the wrath of God. As illustrated in the promise to the church at Philadelphia: "I will also keep thee from the *hour* of temptation, which shall come upon all the world, to try them that dwell upon the earth" (Rev. 3:10, italics added). It is also indicated in 1 Thessalonians 5 that Christians belong to the time designated as "the day" in contrast to "the night" in which the wrath will come. That the wrath of God is only at the end of the tribulation is refuted by the fact that it is mentioned in Revelation 6:17, that is, early in the period.

All pretribulationists concede that the church will experience tribulation throughout its course. The question is whether the church will go through that specific time designated in Scripture as the "great tribulation." It is noteworthy that Ladd does not deal adequately anywhere in his volume with the great theme of the tribulation, although he evidently accepts a literal view of it. The characteristics of judgment of that period are such that they will affect both saved and unsaved, namely, such judgments as earthquakes, pestilence, war, famine, and stars falling from heaven.

Ladd's argument that God will save the church in the tribulation as he saved Israel from the judgments that befell Egypt is its own refutation. No Israelites died in the plague. By contrast, as Ladd himself admits, the tribulation will feature the most awful persecution of saints ever to have occurred in the history of the church, as supported by the multitude of those martyred in Revelation 7 who are said to come out of the great tribulation. While it is true that God can protect those whom He wishes and does protect the 144,000, the Scriptures make clear that the majority of those who trust Christ in the endtime will seal their testimony with their own blood. The whole concept of the saints going triumphantly through the tribulation is not supported by the facts, as only a small portion of them will survive.

RELATION OF POSTTRIBULATIONISM TO DISPENSATIONALISM

Although the recent work by Robert Gundry attempts to support the dispensational interpretation of Scripture while maintaining posttribulationism, his work is an anomaly. He is the first in the history of the church to attempt this approach to posttribulationism.

By contrast, Ladd devotes a whole chapter showing that pretribulationism is built on dispensationalism, and if dispensationalism is proved to be incorrect, pretribulationism falls with it.

Ladd introduces his chapter attacking dispensationalism as the foundation for pretribulationism with these words:

> In this brief chapter, we shall deal with a most important reason used by pretribulationists for refusing to apply the prophecies about the Great Tribulation to the Church. It is so important that it may be called the major premise of dispensationalism. It goes back to J. N. Darby, and is a method of handling the Scriptures which B. W. Newton, one of the earliest and most learned of the Brethren, called "the height of speculative nonsense."[20]

In his discussion of dispensationalism, Ladd departs somewhat from his usual scholarly approach and accuses dispensationalists of holding interpretations that no dispensationalist would support. He defines dispensationalism as "the method of deciding in advance which Scriptures deal with the Church and which Scriptures have to do with Israel, and then to interpret the passages concerned in the light of this single 'division' of the Word."[21] Dispensationalism, however, is not a premise adopted arbitrarily, but a result of the application of literal interpretation of Scripture — which all conservatives recognize is the norm for interpreting the Bible. A literal interpretation of passages dealing with the church and passages dealing with Israel indicates a distinct program, even though there are some similarities. Therefore dispensationalists conclude that there have been various rules of life in Scripture and that it is not proper to apply Scriptures relating to one program to another without sufficient basis.

It has not been possible to deal here with all of Ladd's arguments in support of his conclusions, but it is a fair judgment to say that his opposition to dispensationalism is a major cause for his posttribulational view, and that this is normally the case for posttribulationists. If his premise is correct — that dispensationalism which distinguishes Israel and the church is not a biblical method of interpretation — then Ladd may also be correct in arriving at his posttribulational conclusion. Pretribulationism, however, is clearly based on literal interpretation, which holds that God's program for Israel and His program for the church are not identical.

THE POSTTRIBULATIONAL CONCEPT OF THE BLESSED HOPE

Posttribulationists are not at all agreed as to how the blessed hope fits into the prophetic program, except that they always relate it to the second coming of Christ. Many will agree with Ladd's concluding chapter, in which he expresses the opinion that we should not be so involved in the controversy between pre- and posttribulationism that we neglect our defense of the literalness of the second coming of Christ and the millennium that follows.

In his treatment of the blessed hope, however, it is most significant that Ladd does not expound even briefly the major passages on the blessed hope in the Bible, namely John 14:1-3; 1 Thessalonians 4:13-18; and 1 Corinthians 15:51-58. Instead he quotes an unknown author who uses Titus 2:11-14 to exhort to godly living in expectancy of the Lord's return. Ladd denies that the main force of this passage has to do with the Lord's return and also denies that the passage deals with the rapture. This is pure dogmatism. It does not seem to have occurred to Ladd that the glorious appearing here could very well be the rapture rather than the second coming, as it has only believers in view; to deny that believers will see Christ in His glory at the rapture is to deny the obvious.

It is unfortunate that Ladd repeats the libel that pretribulationism discourages worldwide missions.[22] Many aggressive missionary organizations are pretribulational in their position, and anyone who uses the pretribulational point of view as an argument against missions is certainly violating Scripture. In this, pretribulationists will agree with Ladd while disagreeing that it is an argument against pretribulationism.

In reading the final chapter of Ladd's presentation, it is rather amazing how little is said about the blessed hope itself. Here the problem is that a posttribulational rapture is difficult to harmonize with "the blessed hope" if the church must go through the great tribulation and many, if not most, in the church are martyred. It is hardly a blessed hope that those who survive will be raptured without dying. Far better it would be for them if they had lived out a normal life in a period prior to the rapture and had gone to heaven through death rather than living through the great tribulation. It is rather singular in most posttribulational works that they do not recognize the force of this problem in their own system.

It is also notable that Ladd does not give any reasonable sequence of prophetic events relating to the second coming except that he merges the rapture with the second coming. He does not discuss the problems that this causes premillennialism in regard to populating the millennial earth. He passes over Matthew 25:31-46 without dealing with the problems of posttribulationism. For many pretribulationists, a principal difficulty with the posttribulational view is that it does not resolve the problems that a merger of the rapture and the second coming creates. If posttribulationism is to be credible, its proponents must not dodge their problems but face them.

While futurist posttribulationism tends to be more literal than the views previously examined, it is significant that the same problems emerge. While Ladd tends to interpret prophecy literally, he spiritualizes or ignores the passage whenever this would interfere with posttribulationism. This is illustrated in the spiritualization of the 144,000 in Revelation, which a literal interpretation holds to be a reference to the tribes of Israel. Ladd, however, proposes that this refers to the church, a view inconsistent with his normal use of literal interpretation in prophecy. Likewise Ladd avoids the arguments which contradict his view and, as mentioned above, ignores the problem of the judgment of the nations as well as the order of events described in the Book of Revelation as following the second coming. Accordingly the same defect of inconsistent use of principles of interpretation and faulty induction based upon consideration of only part of the facts is found in the futurist view and others previously considered.

Ladd's plea for tolerance is understandable, and with this many would agree. Fortunately Christians can preach on many truths in agreement although disagreeing on the time of the rapture. However, it remains true that the posttribulational view does not afford a uniform system of prophetic fulfillment related to the second coming, and this is evident by the fact that posttribulationists hardly ever sponsor a prophecy conference or attempt to unify their own school of thought as to the order of endtime events. Their problem is that they do not agree among themselves as to how a posttribulational rapture actually fits the sequence of events related to the second coming.

Notes

[1] George E. Ladd, *The Blessed Hope* (Grand Rapids: Wm. B. Eerdmans Publishing Co., 1956), p. 13.

[2] John F. Walvoord, "A Review of *The Blessed Hope* by George E. Ladd," *Bibliotheca Sacra* 113 (October 1956): 289-307. Some of this previously published material is adapted and used in this chapter.

[3] Ladd, *The Blessed Hope*, p. 19.

[4] Dave MacPherson, *The Incredible Cover-Up* (Plainfield, N. J.: Logos International, 1975).

[5] R. A. Huebner, *The Truth of the Pre-Tribulation Rapture Recovered* (Millington, N. J.: Present Truth Publishers, 1973), p. 14.

[6] Ibid., pp. 66-67.

[7] MacPherson, *Incredible Cover-Up*, pp. 49-52.

[8] John Hooper, "The Church's Expectation," *The Morning Watch* IV (December 1831):321: cited by Huebner, *Truth Recovered*, pp. 22-23.

[9] Huebner, *Truth Recovered*, pp. 19-27.

[10] MacPherson, *Incredible Cover-Up*, pp. 58-60.

[11] Ibid., pp. 59-60.

[12] Huebner, *Truth Recovered*, p. 70.

[13] J. Barton Payne, *The Imminent Appearing of Christ* (Grand Rapids: Wm. B. Eerdmans Publishing Co., 1962), pp. 85-103.

[14] Ladd, *The Blessed Hope*, p. 77.

[15] Ibid., p. 165.

[16] Ibid., p. 77.

[17] Ibid., p. 89.

[18] Ibid., p. 98.

[19] Cf. John F. Walvoord, "Premillennialism and the Tribulation," *Bibliotheca Sacra* 112 (April 1955):97-106.

[20] Ladd, *The Blessed Hope*, p. 130.

[21] Ibid.

[22] Ibid., pp. 146-52. Ladd devotes seven pages to this specious argument.

Chapter 5

Dispensational Posttribulational Interpretation

In the history of the church, a movement can be observed away from an original doctrine of imminency of the Lord's return (as expounded today by J. Barton Payne) toward a nonimminent return of Christ. As earlier chapters have pointed out, while there is confusion in church history on the question of imminency, many of the early church fathers and some of the Protestant Reformers definitely believed that the Lord could come at any time. To accommodate themselves to this point of view, they recognized in their contemporary situation the fulfillment of endtime signs of the second advent.

The twentieth century has seen among posttribulationists a definite trend away from the doctrine of imminency. This is illustrated in the work by George A. Ladd, *The Blessed Hope*,[1] discussed earlier; Ladd definitely believes that there is at least a seven-year period which must be fulfilled before the second coming of Christ.

An entirely new approach to posttribulationism appeared for the first time in the work of Robert H. Gundry, *The Church and the Tribulation*.[2] This work is a further step away from imminency, but is partly built on premises never before used by posttribulationists.

The originator of this new interpretation is a well-known

conservative and premillenarian scholar holding the chairman-ship of the Department of Religious Studies and Philosophy at Westmont College. He has earned the doctor of philosophy degree from Manchester University in England and has written several well-received scholarly publications including *The Use of the Old Testament in St. Matthew's Gospel*[3] and *A Survey of the New Testament.*[4] Although his earlier study in the subject of posttribulationism arose from disagreement with the faculty of Los Angeles Baptist College while he was a student there, his present work reflects the maturity of scholarly studies and his skill as a debater.

In approaching Gundry's arguments for posttribulationism, one encounters exegetical conclusions and logical arguments never before advanced in quite the same way. In a number of particular judgments, if Gundry is right, every previous expositor of the Bible has been wrong. His arguments in other areas, how-ever, have a familiar ring and are derived from traditional post-tribulational thinking.

MAJOR ARGUMENTS OF DISPENSATIONAL POSTTRIBULATIONISM

According to the first chapter of Gundry's book, his work rests on a threefold thesis, namely, that

(1) direct, unquestioned statements of Scripture that Jesus Christ will return after the tribulation and that the first resurrection will occur after the tribulation, coupled with the absence of statements placing similar events before the tribulation, make it natural to place the rapture of the Church after the tribulation; (2) the theological and exegetical grounds for pretribulationism rest on insufficient evidence, *non sequitur* reasoning, and faulty exegesis; (3) positive indications of a posttribulational rapture arise out of a proper exegesis of relevant Scripture passages and derive support from the history of the doctrine.[5]

It is highly important that Gundry's premises include other factors not mentioned specifically here. As a dispensationalist he distinguishes the church and Israel in a manner which has never been expressed in any formal way by previous posttribulationists. It is not too much to say that this premise creates a major difference between his whole argument and that of other post-tribulationists, even though he repeats many traditional argu-ments.

Gundry argues like a skilled debater. He assumes the rightness of posttribulationism when he attempts to harmonize his view with many passages and word studies that form the content of the book. In discussing the tribulation question it is easy for writers on either side to use circular arguments, assuming what they are trying to prove. Gundry does this again and again, as we will show. A number of logical fallacies exist in his presentation.

Much of Gundry's presentation is exegesis of pertinent passages. Here an unusual quality emerges in that he frequently ignores contradictory evidence and presents only the evidence that supports his position. This does not necessarily prove his conclusions wrong, but it raises questions as to why such a one-sided presentation should be offered.

Probably a major aspect of his argument is his attempt to define pivotal issues in such a way that only the posttribulational view could be correct. In this regard the following points can be noted: (1) his attack on the doctrine of imminency as held by pretribulationists and some posttribulationists; (2) his somewhat arbitrary definition of the tribulation period as a time not of divine wrath but only of satanic wrath; (3) his beginning of the "day of the Lord" at Armageddon at the end of the great tribulation; (4) his interpretation of the Olivet Discourse as referring to the church, not Israel; (5) his merging of the various judgments of the righteous into one divine judgment at the second coming; (6) some new and novel suggestions regarding who will enter the millennial kingdom; (7) placing the rapture of the church as occurring just before Armageddon, preceding the second coming of Christ.

The question Gundry raises whether pretribulationism rests "on insufficient evidence, *non sequitur* reasoning, and faulty exegesis" is precisely the question that can be raised by pretribulationists about *his* approach. As his arguments are detailed, an attempt will be made to deal with his view of imminency and the wrath of God and then to survey his exegetical basis for dispensational posttribulationism by examining his exegesis of major passages on which his conclusions stand or

ARGUMENT THAT THE RAPTURE MAY BE ASSUMED
TO OCCUR AT THE SECOND COMING

In his approach to this issue, Gundry states it is only natural to place the rapture after the tribulation, as the second coming of Christ is clearly an event which occurs at that time. This is a familiar argument that most posttribulationists either state or assume. Important as it is, Gundry for some reason does not devote any of his fifteen chapters to a specific discussion of this question. It may be assumed that this is the undergirding thesis that supports the entire book.

At first glance this seems to be a cogent argument which, to a large extent by inference at least, would support posttribulationism. Careful consideration, however, robs this argument of any real force.

In the Old Testament the first and second comings of Christ were often presented in the same revelation. Isaiah 61:1,2 — quoted in part by Christ in the synagogue at Nazareth (Luke 4:16-21) — deals with the first coming of Christ through the phrase in verse 2, "the acceptable year of the LORD." The next phrase, however — "the day of vengeance of our God" — refers to the second coming of Christ. It is significant that Christ in quoting the passage stopped with the portion that dealt with the first coming only.

It would have been quite cogent in the Old Testament to insist that the concept of two comings of the Messiah of Israel was inconceivable. The natural assumption was that there would be only one advent, in which all the prophecies relating to the comings of Christ would be fulfilled. It would have been difficult on the basis of the Old Testament alone to sustain the concept of a first coming and a second coming of Christ separated by thousands of years. Nevertheless, the course of history has supported this very concept. The first coming of Christ took place as predicted, but the portions of Scripture dealing with the second coming are yet to be fulfilled, though exegetically it is impossible to separate them clearly. Historically, fulfillment has demonstrated that there are two distinctive comings. This illustrates that it cannot be presumed that two events presented as a single event actually occur at the same time.

The rapture of the church is presented for the first time in the New Testament. Just as the first and second comings of Christ are mingled in prophetic revelation in the Old Testament, so the rapture of the church and the coming of Christ to set up His kingdom are frequently mingled in the New Testament. Many of the same terms are used; exhortations relating to preparation for the two events are similar.

The lesson to be learned regarding the necessity of separating the first and second comings of Christ is a word of warning that we should not presume that the second coming of Christ includes the rapture. Just as in the Old Testament we can now see the difference between the first and second comings of Christ by studying the particulars that relate to each, so in the New Testament the rapture and Christ's coming to establish His kingdom can be distinguished by itemizing the differences between these two events. This is not in itself an argument for a pretribulation rapture, but it supports the conclusion that the separation of these two events is not illogical or presumptuous. The issue that will someday be settled by a prophetic fulfillment must today be determined exegetically. It is not too much to say that most pretribulationists distinguish the rapture from the coming of Christ to set up His kingdom because the two events are presented with such contrasting details in the New Testament. The posttribulationist cannot throw the burden of proof on the pretribulationist, but must assume his own responsibility to demonstrate that the events are one and the same.

DOES DISPENSATIONALISM PRECLUDE POSTTRIBULATIONISM?

Until Gundry's new approach to posttribulationism was published, it was assumed by practically all pretribulationists and posttribulationists that dispensational interpretation automatically led to pretribulationism. J. Dwight Pentecost, for instance, states, "(1) Posttribulationism must be based on a denial of dispensationalism and all dispensational distinctions. It is only thus that they can place the church in that period which is particularly called 'the time of Jacob's trouble' (Jer. 30:7). (2)

Consequently, the position rests on a denial of the distinction between Israel and the church."[6]

George Ladd in a similar way devotes an entire chapter to dispensationalism in his attack on pretribulationism.[7] He introduces his chapter with these words: "In this brief chapter, we shall deal with the most important reason used by pretribulationists for refusing to apply the prophecies about the Great Tribulation to the Church. It is so important that it may be called the major premise of dispensationalism."[8]

This common assumption by both pretribulationists and posttribulationists is debated by Gundry in his second chapter, entitled "The Dispensational-Ecclesiological Backdrop."[9] In a rather laborious argument Gundry attempts to correct the prevailing view that dispensationalism leads necessarily to pretribulationism so that he can establish a basis for his own dispensational posttribulationism. He admits, "None of the 'mysteries' distinctive of the Church — such as the equality of Jews and Gentiles in one Body, the Church as the bride of Christ, and Christ's indwelling of believers — are ever applied specifically to tribulation saints."[10] He then attempts to dismiss this as being insignificant on the premise that "the burden of proof rather rests on pretribulationists to show that tribulational saints will *not* belong to the Church. . . ."[11] Here Gundry attempts to avoid a major problem of posttribulationism — that the church by that title is never shown to be in the great tribulation. Why does the burden of proof rest on the pretribulationist?

Discussing the church as a mystery, Gundry points out that a number of the truths designated as mysteries — which he properly interprets as New Testament revelation — extend beyond the present age. In this, Gundry is correct. However, the fact that the mystery of lawlessness, the mystery of God, and the mystery of the harlot of Babylon continue into the tribulation is not proof that the church continues in the tribulation. The pretribulationist does not, therefore, argue on the exclusiveness of mystery truth as far as its future fulfillment is concerned; rather, the church as such, because of the various mystery truths related to it, is never found in the tribulation. Even Gundry admits that the translation of the saints — the distinctive feature of the rapture — is declared to be a mystery in 1 Corinthians 15:51,52.[12]

Much like opponents of dispensationalism, Gundry argues that the present age is not completely hidden in the Old Testament. Most dispensationalists concede this. The Old Testament does anticipate a period following the first coming of Christ, though it does not specifically reveal the church age as such. Accordingly the New Testament frequently refers to Old Testament prophecies as being fulfilled in the present age. It is most significant, however, that the particulars mentioned are not those peculiar to the church, but those natural in a post-Calvary situation.

Gundry, like many other posttribulational writers, makes much of the fact that Israel is promised the New Covenant (Jer. 31:31-34). Because this is quoted in Hebrews 8:8-13 as proving that the Mosaic covenant had ceased, Gundry joins amillenarians and some premillenarians in asserting that the covenant with Israel is now being fulfilled in the church.

This seems to me to be mostly a semantic problem. Everyone agrees that when Christ died, He brought in the New Covenant. Everyone agrees that this New Covenant has an application to Israel, an application to the church, and in fact, an application to saints of all ages. Whether the New Covenant is regarded as having a twofold application — one to Israel and the other to the church — or whether it is regarded as two covenants stemming from the death of Christ, it is mostly a problem with words.

The point is that the church is not Israel and does not precisely fulfill the application of the New Covenant to Israel as outlined in Jeremiah 31. The details mentioned in Jeremiah simply are not being fulfilled today, but will be fulfilled in the future millennial kingdom. This whole argument is somewhat extraneous to the issue of pretribulationism versus posttribulationism if the distinction between Israel and the church is maintained. Since Gundry maintains that distinction, it becomes clear that his argument for posttribulationism based on the fulfillment of the New Covenant in the church today loses its force.

In his section on "Dispensational Transitions," an important difference arises between Gundry and other dispensationalists. He admits, "Other things being equal, a clean break between dispensations at Pentecost would make easy the establishing of another clean break between the end of the Church age and the beginning of Daniel's seventieth week."[13] Here Gundry takes the position that just as the change from Israel to the church took place over a prolonged period of transition, so there will be a prolonged transition from the church into the millennium. Most dispensationalists agree that there is a transitional period in the Book of Acts. However, this does not in itself prove that there will be a transitional period at the end of the church age. The Book of Acts is clear in mentioning both the church and Israel, but in the tribulation the church is not mentioned at all, and the burden of proof is on the posttribulationist. Dispensationalists grant that there are many similarities between the church and Israel. The very fact of salvation binds all saints of all ages together. This does not in itself, however, make Israel as an entity and the church as an entity one and the same.

The crux of Gundry's argument is in his section on "The Economy of the Tribulation." He introduces this with the statement, "If the Church is to go through the tribulation, God will work simultaneously with two groups of covenant people, Israel and the Church."[14] Pretribulationists can agree with Gundry on this point without agreeing with his posttribulationism. The point is, as Gundry himself admits, Israel is in unbelief in this period, and Israelites who believe would become part of the church, not a separate redeemed people. Gundry himself says that "the tribulation knows only one group of redeemed people, the Church."[15] Here is precisely the point: the redeemed people in the tribulation are described as saved Israelites and saved Gentiles, not as "the Church." This is one of the numerous instances in which Gundry assumes what he is trying to prove.

In his summary Gundry again contends that the dispensation of the church does not end with a clean break, but continues throughout the tribulation period. Here he argues from the premise that there is no clean break to the conclusion that the church is in the tribulation. Logically it should be just the reverse. The transition should be demonstrated by proving that the church is in the tribulation. Until this is established, it is impossible to prove that there is a transition.

SUMMARY

Gundry makes clear at the start that his approach is different from that of any posttribulationist in the past, though he also adopts many familiar arguments. Gundry is, first of all, a dispensationalist who distinguishes Israel from the church. To maintain his posttribulationism, however, he attempts to divorce himself from what has been considered normal dispensationalism, which calls for a sharp break between the church age and the period between the church and the second coming of Christ. It is essential to Gundry's position that he makes the transition gradual, not marked by an event like the rapture which abruptly terminates the church age. While agreeing with dispensationalists on many points, he differs with them where it would conflict with his posttribulationism. The real problem Gundry faces is harmonizing his dispensational point of view with posttribulational interpretation in general.

Although Gundry attempts to follow consistently the principle of normal or literal interpretation of prophecy, the same problems found in other forms of posttribulationism soon become evident. Gundry abandons literal interpretation when it would lead to a contradiction of posttribulationism. Further in Gundry, perhaps more than in any other posttribulationist, the selection of facts in a given passage without facing contradictory evidence is a glaring, logical fault which permeates his discussion. This leads to an induction based upon selected facts instead of all the facts bearing upon the doctrine.

Notes

[1] George A. Ladd, *The Blessed Hope* (Grand Rapids: Wm. B. Eerdmans Publishing Co., 1956).

[2] Robert H. Gundry, *The Church and the Tribulation* (Grand Rapids: Zondervan Publishing House, 1973).

[3] Leiden: E. J. Brill, 1967.

[4] Grand Rapids: Zondervan Publishing House, 1970.

[5] Gundry, *The Church and the Tribulation*, p. 10.

[6] J. Dwight Pentecost, *Things to Come* (Findlay, Ohio: Dunham Publishing Co., 1958), p. 164.

[7] Ladd, *The Blessed Hope*, pp. 130-36.

[8] Ibid., p. 130.
[9] Gundry, *The Church and the Tribulation,* pp. 12-28.
[10] Ibid., p. 13.
[11] Ibid.
[12] Ibid., p. 14.
[13] Ibid., p. 19.
[14] Ibid., p. 23.
[15] Ibid., p. 24.

Chapter 6

Posttribulational Denial of Imminency and Wrath

Taking advantage of the fact that the word *imminent* is not a scriptural word, but an induction from scriptural facts, Robert Gundry attempts to deny the imminency of the rapture by re-definition of the term. The word *imminent*, of course, is not used in Scripture, but has normally been considered to represent the view that the rapture could occur at any time. Some posttribulationists, such as J. Barton Payne, agree that the Lord could come at any moment and that there are no necessary intervening events. This is the proper meaning of the concept of imminence.

Gundry, in his support of posttribulationism, attempts to solve the problem by redefining the English word. "We should first of all note a lack of identity between belief in imminence on the one hand and pretribulationism on the other," he states. "By common consent imminence means that so far as we know no predicted event will *necessarily* precede the coming of Christ. The concept incorporates three essential elements: suddenness, unex-pectedness or incalculability, and a possibility of occurrence at any moment. But these elements would require only that Christ *might* come before the tribulation, not that He must. Imminence would only raise the possibility of pretribulationism on a sliding scale with mid- and posttribulationism. It is singularly strange that the most popularly cherished argument for pretribulationism should suffer such an obvious and critical limitation."[1]

An observation could be made on this preliminary statement that "it is singularly strange" that a capable scholar should advance such a slanted definition of imminence. It is true that there is a lack of identity between belief in imminence and pretribulationism. But this is true only when a posttribulationist like J. Barton Payne spiritualizes the tribulation so that the rapture could occur any day. It is not true when a sequence of well-defined prophetic events intervenes between the present and the rapture of the church, as Gundry holds.

According to Gundry, there is a definite sequence of events — including the great tribulation — which precedes the second coming of Christ and therefore imminence in the sense of an event that could occur at any time is actually impossible. Gundry's statement that "these elements would require only that Christ *might* come before the tribulation, not that He must" is not true.[2] Gundry's view absolutely demands that there be major world events occurring before the rapture. In no sense is this a proper definition of imminence. For Gundry there is no possibility of the rapture occurring any day because he outlines a series of events (including the great tribulation) that must literally take place before the church can be raptured.

The doctrine of imminence, to be sure, does not date the rapture, and it is no embarrassment to the pretribulationist that nineteen hundred years have elapsed since the promise was given. Some events predicted were not clearly related to the rapture, such as the destruction of Jerusalem in A.D. 70; at the time of its prediction this event could have either preceded or followed the rapture. Fulfillment, however, has indicated that it would precede the rapture. This is quite different, however, from assuming that the rapture after the tribulation is a possibility.

Pretribulationists believe there will be no rapture at the end of the tribulation, and saints living at that time will go into the millennial kingdom in their natural bodies. Posttribulationists, however, hold that there will be no rapture before the final events described in the great tribulation, and the rapture is a part of the conclusion of the tribulation and synonymous with the second coming of Christ to the earth.

Accordingly, when Gundry says, "The limitation of the imminence aside, an expectant attitude toward the Lord's return does not contradict the posttribulational belief in necessarily preceding events,"[3] it is a dogmatic statement unsupported by facts. Gundry in effect admits that the concept of imminency tends to contradict posttribulationism. The doctrine of imminence is incompatible with the posttribulational view, unless one holds, like Payne, that the tribulation should be spiritualized and considered as already fulfilled.

The real issue, as pretribulationists state it, is that the hope offered them in the New Testament is the hope of the rapture before the tribulation, not the hope of survival through the tribulation. Thus, when the rapture is presented without any detailed events preceding it, the fulfillment of the hope of the rapture is properly regarded as an imminent event that *must* occur before the detailed prophecies leading up to Christ's return to set up His kingdom. Gundry is attempting to solve the problem by redefining the word *imminent* to make it apply to his concept of the second coming — which in no sense is imminent, but preceded by very dramatic and specific world events.

In attempting to redefine *imminence*, Gundry offers a study of various words used for "expectation" in the Bible. Not only is his study slanted in an attempt to support his version of imminence, but the argument as presented is irrelevant, though to the unwary impressive. The doctrine of pretribulationism, as well as its concept of imminence as applying to an any-day rapture, does not depend on definitions of words, but on the context in which the words are used. Gundry confuses the whole issue and begs the question by putting together passages as relating to both the rapture and the second coming simply because the same word is used in both. This does not prove that they refer to the same event or to expectancy of the same event. Gundry admits at the conclusion of his word study, "Since the words for expectancy do not resolve the question of imminence one way or the other, their contexts become decisive."[4] One wonders why he goes to such great lengths in a word study when he concedes it does not prove anything.

What is true of Gundry's treatment of the word study also

applies to the discussion of the contexts. Here Gundry begs the question by assuming that if exhortations are given to watch in connection with both the rapture and the coming of Christ after the tribulation, this proves the expectancy is the same. Obviously the question in each case concerns to whom the exhortation is given. While the church may be watching for the rapture, those in the great tribulation may be watching for the second coming. Gundry's argument seems impressive, but it actually does not prove what he is attempting to prove.

In the first century the concept of imminency was qualified by certain predictions relating to individuals such as Peter and Paul. Peter was told that he would die an old man (John 21:18,19). Paul was informed that he had a great ministry ahead in Corinth (Acts 18:9-11), which actually continued for eighteen months; for a brief time Paul could conclude that the rapture would not occur. Later the Lord revealed to Paul in custody in Jerusalem that he would live long enough to visit Rome (Acts 23:11), which occurred two full years later (Acts 24:27). As far as the church at large was concerned, the information given to Paul and Peter did not deter their belief in imminency because on a given day few would know whether Paul or Peter was still alive, and most of them were not informed about the predictions.

No such problem exists today in the doctrine of imminency. There is no authoritative revelation of intervening events. To use these temporary problems in the first century to deny imminency today is not reasonably justified.

Much of Gundry's argument depends on assumptions he does not prove, such as the premise that the Olivet Discourse is addressed to the church. This is sufficiently important to merit special treatment later. There is an obvious difference between exhortations in the Olivet Discourse and those addressed to the church in the present age. This difference is that the Olivet Discourse is an exhortation to watch *after* the signs have been fulfilled, including the beginning of the great tribulation, whereas in the rapture passages believers in the present age are encouraged to look for the coming of the Lord without respect to any signs and are given no signs for the rapture itself. The situation is dramatically different. When Gundry gets through, while it is impressive to those who do not know the intricacies of this argument, he actually offers no proof in support of his major premise that the Bible puts endtime events before the rapture.

Concepts of imminency have varied in the history of doctrine and theological studies. Some posttribulationists do hold to a literal imminency, that is, that Christ's second coming can occur at any time as Luther and Calvin did in their latter years. J. Barton Payne accomplished this by spiritualizing events leading up to the second coming.[5]

Gundry has an entirely different viewpoint, however, as he takes the events of the great tribulation literally and must necessarily interpose these before his posttribulational rapture. Accordingly, while Payne can properly refer to his view as an imminent return of Christ, Gundry cannot do so if the word is traditionally defined. Gundry's statement, "A tribulation interval no more destroys expectancy than the necessary delays during the Apostolic Age," is pure dogmatism that he does not even attempt to support by argument.[6]

Gundry's presentation makes clear that if one believes in his form of posttribulationism, the hope of the Lord's return before the great tribulation is a vain illusion, and what we are looking for is not the Lord's coming but the great tribulation. Because this is hardly a "blessed hope," pretribulationists continue to insist that their viewpoint is quite different in its expectation from the posttribulationists'. If there are well-defined events that must occur before the rapture of the church, as Gundry holds, then the concept of imminency no longer is properly applied to the rapture.

DENIAL OF DIVINE WRATH IN THE GREAT TRIBULATION

Gundry begins his chapter on "Wrath and Rapture" by accusing pretribulationists of wrongly appealing to fear of the coming great tribulation. He states, "Sometimes the argument is so stated as to be marred by an appeal of fear."[7] In a similar way Oswald T. Allis in his attempted refutation of pretribulationism puts all his arguments under one subpoint, "Pretribulationism Appeals to Unworthy Motives" (italicized in original), and debates the entire pretribulational view on this basis.[8]

Is it an unworthy motive to desire to escape the great tribulation? Actually it is no more so than the desire to escape hell. The point in either case is not our desire or wishes, but the question as to what the Scriptures promise. Pretribulationists hope to escape the great tribulation because it is expressly a time of divine judgment upon a world that has rejected Christ. But the Scriptures also reveal the great tribulation as a time of satanic wrath against Israel and believers in Christ who are living at that time. The great tribulation is a time of both divine wrath and satanic wrath. Pretribulationists believe that the rapture passages promise a deliverance which occurs before this final period of trial overtakes a wicked world.

Gundry's approach to the subject of wrath and rapture is an attempt to make the great tribulation a time of satanic wrath, but not a time of divine wrath with a view to relieving the severity of the period in relation to believers. His argument here is confused. His leading heading is "The Exemption of All Saints from Divine Wrath."[9] This argument, common among posttribulationists, is built upon the false assumption that if the tribulation is not a time of divine wrath, then Christians will escape the severity of the period.

Gundry is wrong on both counts. Not only do saints suffer severely in the great tribulation, but it is also a time of divine wrath. Gundry's whole approach fails to do justice to the facts and is faulty in its logic.

Even if the great tribulation were purely a time of satanic wrath, why would this assure that Christians escape? Job certainly did not escape satanic wrath once God permitted Satan to afflict him. It should be clear to any reader that saints in the great tribulation suffer severely as the objects of satanic wrath, and that the world as a whole suffers severely because it is the object of divine wrath.

Most conservative expositors agree that the great tribulation in Scripture is definitely revealed to be a time of satanic wrath. This is expressly stated in Revelation 12:12, and Satan's wrath is seen in the persecution of believers in Christ, evidence in itself that Christians do not escape. Many martyrs are seen in Revelation 6:9-11, and most conservative interpreters regard Revelation 7:9-17 as referring also to those who die as martyrs.

It is typical of posttribulationists that they attempt to water down and weaken in every possible way the extent of the sufferings of the great tribulation as they relate to the saints. Gundry arbitrarily moves Revelation 7:9-17 out of the tribulation and into the eternal state with no contextual support whatever. This viewpoint is somewhat necessary to posttribulationists because they contend the church goes through the tribulation, and if the great majority is martyred they will, of course, not go through the tribulation.

Accordingly, even a relatively literal posttribulationist like Gundry has to avoid the full force of prophecy as it relates to the trials of the saints in the great tribulation. Whatever trials do eventuate, both posttribulationists and pretribulationists agree, result from satanic wrath rather than from divine wrath. Gundry, however, attempts to support the idea that all the trials of the tribulation are simply satanic in their origin and not a matter of divine wrath upon a wicked world.

Gundry's thinking on this point is cloudy because if the world is the object of satanic wrath, then the church going through the tribulation experiences it also. This position assures the church no escape from martyrdom if it has to go through the tribulation.

That the great tribulation is a time of divine wrath, however, is expressly stated in Scripture, and Gundry is wrong when he denies it. The sixth seal introduces, according to Revelation 6:17, "the great day of his wrath," but the preceding seals record devastating divine judgments. War, famine, death, and martyrdom occur in the first five seals of Revelation 6. Many expositors also hold that the sixth and seventh seals are part of the great tribulation and that the seventh seal includes the trumpet judgments and the vial judgments. Gundry claims that the sixth seal occurs at the end of the tribulation and that the seventh seal deals with the second coming itself. Thus he concludes, "God's wrath will not stretch throughout the whole tribulation."[10] This rather dogmatic statement does not take into account what has already been described in the preceding seal judgments. While the climax of the wrath of God may very well be introduced by the sixth seal, it is by no means the beginning of the wrath of God upon the world.

Christ Himself declared the entire great tribulation a time of unprecedented trouble. As stated in Matthew 24:15-22, the great tribulation begins with the breaking of the Jewish covenant. This occurs at the beginning of the last three and a half years preceding the second coming of Christ and is called "the time of Jacob's trouble" in Jeremiah 30:7. The same period is described in Revelation 13:5 as the last forty-two months preceding the second coming.

Many conservative expositors who take this literally recognize this as a period of satanic wrath beginning with Satan's being cast out of heaven, according to Revelation 12:9. Chronologically this begins the last three and a half years before the second advent. It is clear, however, from the nature of the judgments poured out that these last three and a half years are also a time of divine wrath upon the earth. This is evident by the disturbances in heaven, great earthquakes, and the catastrophes described under the trumpet judgments and the vial judgments. All of this cannot be compacted to be fulfilled on a given day such as Armageddon; rather it describes the entire process of the three and a half years leading up to Armageddon. Armageddon is the climax immediately preceding the second coming of Christ.

The entire period of three and a half years is so awful that Christ Himself predicted that if it were not terminated by His second coming, the whole human race would be destroyed (Matt. 24:22). Gundry's attempt to soften the force of these divine judgments prior to Armageddon — to relieve it of the character of being a period of divine wrath — is motivated by his interpretation of 1 Thessalonians 5, where the church is promised deliverance from the time of wrath — a view which will be discussed in full later. His point of view, however, is simply not supported by the facts of the Book of Revelation, which plainly indicate that the wrath of God is poured out in the world throughout the entire period of the great tribulation, even though it is also clear that it becomes increasingly severe as it approaches the second advent.

That these endtime judgments extend over a period of time is brought out by the fact that Christ Himself says the great tribulation will begin with the abomination of desolation, which occurs three and one-half years before His second coming (Matt. 24:15). It is also supported by Revelation 9:5, where the duration of the fifth trumpet alone is said to be five months. The catastrophe pictured in the seals, trumpets, and vials extends over the entire three-and-a-half-year period leading up to the second coming of Christ. Some expositors even extend it over the entire seven-year period preceding the second advent.

Gundry is forced to an extreme and untenable position by trying to bring the church *through* the great tribulation without *experiencing* great tribulation. His position is further complicated in that satanic wrath is expressly against believers and the people of Israel, while divine wrath is against the world as a whole. In some sense, Gundry is arguing against himself, because if it is a period of satanic wrath and the church is its object, then one cannot conclude that the church is delivered from tribulation while passing through it.

A sober evaluation of the nature of the catastrophes that occur in the last three and a half years preceding the second coming of Christ indicate they could not all be brought about by Satan himself. They are pictured in Scripture as judgments directed primarily against the wicked in which the righteous are unfortunately also caught. Satan has no controversy with the wicked and is attempting to vent his wrath only against the people of God, not against his own subjects. By contrast, the wrath of God is worldwide in its extent and deals with an earth largely Christ-rejecting and worshiping the world ruler of the endtime.

Though many believers are martyred in the great tribulation, most of those who perish are actually unbelievers. Revelation 6:8 indicates that a fourth part of the earth perishes. These people do not die because of Satan, but because of divine judgments in the form of war, pestilence, and famine.

It may be concluded that the whole theory that the tribulation is purely and simply a time of satanic wrath and not of divine wrath is both inaccurate and actually irrelevant because it has nothing to do with the question of whether the church goes through the period. Some of Gundry's contentions actually fight against the conclusion he is trying to reach.

Nevertheless Gundry's position on this point is critical to his whole system. The church is promised deliverance from the day of divine wrath, according to 1 Thessalonians 5:9. This is why Gundry attempts to support the concept that the period is not a day of divine wrath. However, his viewpoint requires him to support both the idea that the church is not the object of the individual wrath of God (which is disputed by none) and the idea that the church does not even enter the *time* of divine wrath and is removed before that time begins. This is why he holds that the wrath of God begins only at Armageddon at the end of the great tribulation.

This unusual and extreme position becomes an untenable hypothesis when all the facts are considered. If the church is going through the great tribulation, it will go through the time of wrath designed not to purge the church, but to deal with the Christ-rejecting world. The problem is that such catastrophes as war and famine, as indicated in the second and third seals of Revelation 6, do not single out unsaved people only. A fourth of the earth's population will be destroyed, as indicated in the fourth seal, and this also extends the divine wrath to the entire human race. The prospect of a church's going triumphantly through the great tribulation relatively untouched is not supported in the prophecies of the Book of Revelation, as indicated by the martyrs in chapters 6 and 7.

The content of Revelation 7:9-17, which Gundry attempts to place after the second advent without any supporting evidence, is another plain indication of the extent of the saints' martyrdom in the tribulation. These passages clearly give a picture of heaven, not of the millennial earth (compare Rev. 7:11 with Rev. 5:8). Saints are no longer in their natural bodies as those who have survived the tribulation, but rather are presented as those who have died in the tribulation and who "came out of great tribulation." To project this scene into the period after the second coming to either the millennium or the eternal state has no exegetical support in the context.

Though the Book of Revelation does not have a strictly chronological order, the context is relevant. In chapter 7 the contrast is between the 144,000 of Israel, who are sealed and protected through the great tribulation, and the multitude of the saved which no man can number, who do not survive the tribulation and who are not sealed. It would seem that the burden of proof is on Gundry to prove that this is not a tribulational situation because the implication is that is belongs to this period even though Revelation 7 is a parenthesis. It is most significant that the word *church* is not used at all, and the saints are described simply as those who have been saved by the blood of the Lamb and who have come out of great trials.

Gundry's conclusion that the great tribulation is not a time of divine wrath rests only upon his dogmatic statements, not upon evidence presented. If the church must go through this period, probably the majority would not be delivered, but martyred. His attempt to support the idea that this is a period of satanic persecution, but not of divine judgment, is shattered by the evidence of what occurs in the seals, trumpets, and vials. Inasmuch as his thesis — that this is only a time of satanic wrath — is unsupported, to the same extent his whole argument is unsupported.

A major problem with posttribulationists is that they must get the church through the tribulation relatively unscathed, but the only way they can do this is to deny or ignore the plain teachings of the Book of Revelation on this subject. The martyrs of Revelation 6 and 7 are eloquent in their testimony; significantly there is no evidence that these martyrs are related to the church as such. The only way Gundry can support his position on this point is to be selective in his material and to ignore the major prophecies relating to the great tribulation. If his argument here is faulty and unsupported, so also his conclusions are unsupported.

EXEGETICAL PREMISES OF DISPENSATIONAL POSTTRIBULATIONISM

Most of Gundry's important arguments for posttribulationism are based on exegesis of key passages, such as the Olivet Discourse in Matthew 24–25; the Upper Room Discourse in John 13–17 and particularly John 14:1-3; 1 Thessalonians 4:13-18; 1 Thessalonians 5:1-11; 2 Thessalonians 2:1-12; 1 Corinthians 15:51-58; and the entire Book of Revelation.

Though Gundry weaves the facts of these passages into his various arguments throughout his book, probably the most direct way of dealing with the theological issues involved is to turn to these passages and consider them exegetically. Central to his argument is that the Olivet Discourse concerns primarily the church, not Israel, and this concept will be considered next.

Notes

[1] Robert H. Gundry, *The Church and the Tribulation* (Grand Rapids: Zondervan Publishing House, 1973), p. 29.

[2] Ibid.

[3] Ibid.

[4] Ibid., p. 33.

[5] J. Barton Payne, *The Imminent Appearing of Christ* (Grand Rapids: Wm. B. Eerdmans, 1962).

[6] Gundry, *The Church and the Tribulation*, p. 43.

[7] Ibid., p. 44.

[8] Oswald T. Allis, *Prophecy and the Church* (Philadelphia: Presbyterian and Reformed Publishing Co., 1945), p. 207.

[9] Gundry, *The Church and the Tribulation*, p. 44.

[10] Ibid., p. 77.

Chapter 7

Do the Gospels Reveal a
Posttribulational Rapture?

The major weaknesses of dispensational posttribulationism are found in the exegesis advanced to support this new
doctrine. It is in this aspect that dispensational posttribulationism
fails to persuade either pretribulationists or traditional posttribulationists.

Though the treatment of various passages on the surface
seems to be scriptural because of the numerous arguments and
Scripture citations included, two pervading weaknesses can be
noted in the exegesis: (1) the argument is selective, ignoring
contradictory evidence in the passage itself; (2) the argument
frequently either misstates or ignores the main thrust of the passage. These are weighty and important objections even if they are
made against what seems on the surface to be a scholarly argument. These objections against dispensational posttribulationism
are also often valid against other forms of posttribulationism.

Undoubtedly an important aspect of posttribulationism, regardless of which school of interpretation is followed, is the question of the doctrine of the rapture in the Gospel of Matthew. For
the most part, Mark and Luke do not contribute to the argument,
and the Gospel of John falls in a different category. In Matthew,
the principal chapters pertaining to the tribulation question are
13, 24, and 25, embracing two major discourses of Christ.

Matthew 13 comes at an important juncture in the Gospel, where Christ has been rejected by the Jews as their Messiah; in response Christ pronounces severe judgment on them for their unbelief. In keeping with the main thrust of the whole Gospel of Matthew, which is to explain why the predicted Old Testament kingdom was not fulfilled in Christ's first coming, Matthew 13 has as its dominant subject a sweeping revelation of the general characteristics of the period between the first coming and the second coming of Christ, a subject almost completely ignored in the Old Testament. Accordingly, in seven parables our Lord describes the various aspects of the period between the first and second comings of Christ.[1]

The position of dispensational posttribulationism is stated briefly by Gundry in what he calls "Excursus on the Consummation of the Age."[2] Most pretribulationists and posttribulationists agree that Matthew 13 is dealing with the entire interadvent age from the first coming of Christ to His second coming to establish His kingdom. A few pretribulationists have tried to make it coterminous with the church age, but this is an unnecessary and an unsupported conclusion; at this point in the revelation Christ has not even introduced the doctrine of the rapture, much less expounded it. Even the church as such is not introduced until Matthew 16.

Gundry follows other posttribulationists, however, in singling out the parable of the wheat and the tares as evidence for a posttribulational rapture. As Matthew 13:30 states clearly, at the time of the harvest the tares are gathered first, and then the wheat is gathered into the barn. Gundry, like most other posttribulationists, makes much of the fact that the wheat is gathered *after* the tares — which fact, he holds, corresponds to the second coming of Christ to set up His kingdom. This contradicts the order of the pretribulational rapture, in which believers are gathered out first. Like other posttribulationists, however, Gundry ignores the parable of the dragnet in Matthew 13:47-50 in which the exact opposite order is indicated. There, according to verse 48, the good fish representing believers are gathered into vessels, and then the bad fish are thrown away.

It should be obvious under these circumstances that these parables are not trying to set up a precise order, but rather the fact of separation as brought out so clearly in Matthew 13:49,50. At the second coming of Christ to establish His kingdom, it may well be that the wicked are judged first, and then the righteous are gathered into His kingdom. This presumes, however, that the rapture has occurred earlier. If a posttribulational rapture is assumed, however, they have a real problem with this event related to the second coming, as obviously Christ comes to earth first and then the wicked are judged. If they desire to press this order, it becomes a problem to posttribulationism, but not to pretribulationism. The pretribulationist is unconcerned in interpreting this passage as to whether the unsaved are gathered first or the saved are gathered first. Either order is admissable at the time of the second coming of Christ to establish His kingdom. Gundry is actually fighting a straw man here, for pretribulationists do not claim that these parables describe the rapture.

One of Gundry's peculiarities is his opposition to the view that all the wicked will be judged at the time of the second coming of Christ. He states, "The gathering and burning of the wicked must not include the entire unsaved population of the earth, else none would be left to be the goats in the judgment of the nations (in the pretribulational scheme) or to enter the millennium (the posttribulational scheme). We may solve this problem by limiting the sphere of judgment to false disciples in the kingdom."[3]

Although this question is not important to the pretribulational argument, it is crucial to Gundry's approach to posttribulationism. Due to his peculiar interpretation of Matthew 25 — in which he places the judgment of the nations at the *end* of the millennium — he is forced to take unusual steps to evade the problems this creates, one of which is his partial judgment on the wicked at the second coming. Virtually all premillenarians and amillenarians, whether posttribulational or pretribulational, hold that *all* the wicked living on earth are judged at the second coming of Christ.

The Scriptures seem to make plain that all the wicked perish at the time of the second coming, and only persons who are born again enter the kingdom. This is the background of Christ's conversation with Nicodemus in John 3:3-5. There Nicodemus, on the basis of Old Testament revelation, is chided for not knowing that a person has to be born again to enter the kingdom of God. Though a spiritual kingdom was in view in Christ's words, it was also associated in Nicodemus' mind with the coming kingdom of God on earth.

The Book of Revelation makes quite plain that there will be only two classes of citizens spiritually during the great tribulation, the saved and the lost (Rev. 13:8). All who are lost will worship the beast or the world ruler of the endtime; according to Revelation 14:9-11, all who worship the beast will suffer eternal torment. Revelation 19:21 tells us that all the armies of the world that fight Christ at His second coming will be destroyed.

If most expositors are correct that the judgment of the nations occurs at the time of the second advent of Christ, it follows that the goats representing all the unsaved are cast into everlasting fire. It should become apparent that the dispensational posttribulationism advanced by Gundry is built on untenable and strange interpretations which even his fellow posttribulationists do not follow. One can only conclude that the exegetical basis for his posttribulationism is faulty.

In a word, Matthew 13 does not discuss the doctrine of the rapture at all, and there is absolutely nothing in this passage that would contradict the pretribulational view. The arguments advanced by Gundry are not only inadequately supported, but irrelevant.

THE RAPTURE IN MATTHEW 24

A most crucial argument advanced by Gundry for his dispensational posttribulationism is based on his exegesis of Matthew 24,25. His views are somewhat novel, but unquestionably these two chapters have had a bearing on posttribulationism as a whole. It is most unfortunate for his argument that the same problems faced in exegesis of other passages surface here. Gundry again is selective in his material, choosing only what supports his view and ignoring contradictory evidence; he tends to evade the obvious subject matter of the passage.

Gundry's approach is to debate at great length whether the Olivet Discourse is addressed to the church or to Israel. He asks the question, "To what group of redeemed do the Jewish saints addressed by Jesus and represented by the apostles belong, Israel or the Church?"[4]

The question as to whom the Gospels, including the Olivet Discourse, are addressed, has been mishandled by both dispensationalists and nondispensationalists. Obviously all the Gospels were written after Pentecost and they record material pertinent, in one respect or another, to those living in the church age. The actual subject matter of any point in revelation, however, has to be determined exegetically, not by sweeping categories. Thus, while Matthew is addressed primarily to Jewish Christians to explain why the kingdom was not brought in at Christ's first coming, it also includes reference to the church in Matthew 16.

Actually all four Gospels deal with three dispensations, sometimes reaching back into the Law and expounding the meaning of the law of Moses, sometimes looking forward to the millennial kingdom, a future age, and sometimes dealing with the present age, the church. The question as to whom any particular passage is addressed cannot be settled by the fact that it was given to the disciples, because they represent in some sense both Israel and the church. The issue must be settled on the subject matter, much in the same way that a person living in the present age can go back into the Old Testament and read portions addressed to someone else that may have application to spiritual issues today.

Gundry's entire argument in his chapter on the Olivet Discourse, which concerns itself mainly with this question, is largely irrelevant. What is most important is that Gundry completely ignores and does not even notice what the subject of the passage is.[5] According to Mark 13:3, four of the disciples, Peter, James, John, and Andrew, asked Christ three questions. These are stated in Matthew 24:3: (1) "When shall these things be?"; (2) "What shall be the sign of thy coming?"; and (3) What shall be the sign "of the end of the age?" (NASB). It is difficult to understand why Gundry in his chapter on the Olivet Discourse should not even mention the questions being answered. In an analysis of the Olivet Discourse, the subject matter is more important than the question of to whom it was stated.

To the pretribulationist it is obvious that the rapture is not in view in this passage. Up to this point the disciples had had no instruction on this subject. They did not even clearly understand the difference between the first and second comings of Christ. Their questions indicated that they were first of all concerned about the destruction of Jerusalem which Christ had predicted in Matthew 24:2, as this obviously signaled some tremendous event. Christ did not deal with this first question in Matthew, but He did answer it in Mark and Luke; and, of course, the prophecy was fulfilled in the destruction of Jerusalem in A.D. 70.

The second and third questions are the same. The coming of Christ and the end of the age are coterminous, and the answer to the one is the answer to the other. Here again it is questionable whether the disciples clearly understood at the time that there would be a time period between the first and second comings of Christ. What they were talking about was Christ's coming to establish His kingdom and the end of the age preceding it, during which, from their viewpoint, they could still be living. Accordingly the nature of the question is such that the church is not in view, nor is the rapture introduced. In a word, the disciples wanted to know the signs leading up to the establishment of the millennial kingdom.

In His answer Christ first stated the general signs of the period leading up to the second coming (Matt. 24:4-14). This coincides with Matthew 13. Then he gave them the specific sign of the beginning of the great tribulation three and one-half years before His second coming, signaled by the abomination of desolation (Matt. 24:15). The period of great tribulation will end, according to Christ, with His glorious second coming. Though Christ answered the questions of the disciples, He did not give all the details, many of which were supplied later in Revelation 4–18.

The question raised by posttribulationists as to why Christ did not clearly delineate here a pretribulation rapture is answered simply by the fact that this was not His subject. If in the Old Testament the frequent references to the first and second comings of Christ make no clear distinction of the two events, why should Christ be obligated here to explain an event He had not even introduced? Christ chose to introduce this in the Upper Room the night before His crucifixion. Nevertheless the full exposition of the

rapture was not to be given until later through the apostle Paul.
The reasons are fairly obvious. The disciples were in no mood
or situation to understand such a new doctrine. They did not even
comprehend the concept of the church at this time, even though it
had been announced. How could they be expected to understand
the distinction between a pretribulation rapture and the posttribulational second coming to establish the kingdom of Christ on
earth? The silence of Christ on the subject of the rapture here
should be understandable in view of the subject matter and the
total situation. If God did not see fit to reveal many other aspects
of the special purpose He has for the church, the body of Christ,
until the Pauline letters, it is not strange that the subject of the
rapture should not be expounded in Matthew 24.

Despite the fact the subject matter does not concern the
rapture, it is not unusual for both pretribulationists and posttribulationists to attempt to read the rapture truth into this passage. Here the hermeneutical rule that the context must determine interpretation should be applied, and later revelation should
not be read into earlier revelation unless the text itself justifies
this.

The question as to whether the Olivet Discourse specifically
discusses the rapture is asked by Gundry, "Where in the Olivet
Discourse are we to place the rapture? There is no mention of a
rapture prior to the tribulation."[6] All agree that there is no
mention of a pretribulational rapture in this passage. The important question remains, however, whether there is mention of a
posttribulational rapture.

Two passages in the Olivet Discourse are usually cited by
posttribulationists, and Gundry goes along with their interpretation. According to Matthew 24:31, "They shall gather together
his elect from the four winds, from one end of heaven to the other."
Mark 13:27 states, "And then shall he send his angels, and shall
gather together his elect from the four winds, from the uttermost
part of the earth to the uttermost part of heaven."

It should be stated first that these verses cause no problem
whatever to a pretribulationist. All pretribulationists agree that at
the time Christ comes to set up His kingdom, the elect will be
gathered from heaven and earth to participate in the millennial

kingdom. Whether these elect refer only to the elect of Israel or include both saved Israelites and Gentiles and the church, all agree that this gathering will take place with the establishment of the millennial kingdom.

The question is not whether there will be such a gathering. The question is whether this gathering is the rapture of the church. Here the evidence is missing. There is a conspicuous absence of any reference to a translation of living saints or of any specific reference to the resurrection of the church in any passage in the Old or New Testaments that clearly refers to Christ's coming to establish His kingdom. Thus, for a posttribulationist to claim this passage is to beg the question, to assume what he is trying to prove. Inasmuch as the most important and distinctive aspect of the rapture is the translation of living saints, this becomes the key question. Pretribulationists conclude that this passage does not contradict their point of view and does not support the posttribulational argument.

An argument advanced by Alexander Reese and adopted by Gundry is that the references in Matthew 24:40,41 should be interpreted as referring to the rapture. These verses state, "Then shall two be in the field; the one shall be taken, and the other left. Two women shall be grinding at the mill; the one shall be taken and the other left."

Here both Gundry and Reese violate the rule that the context should determine the interpretation of a passage.[7] Both Gundry and Reese concede that the context deals with judgment such as characterized the time of Noah. According to Matthew 24:39 those living at that time "knew not until the flood came, and took them all away, so shall also the coming of the Son of man be." Those taken away were taken away in judgment.

Gundry and Reese note that the words "shall be taken" in verses 40 and 41 are the translation of *paralambano*, a different word from the one used in verse 39. Reese, however, erroneously states, "It is a good word; a word used exclusively in the sense of 'take away with' or 'receive' or 'take *home*.' "[8]

The truth is that this is a common word used with many connotations, and it is not true, as Reese and Gundry state, that it is always used in a friendly sense. The same word is used in John

19:16 of taking Christ to Calvary for crucifixion, an express instance of taking one away to judgment. Accordingly the use of this word is indecisive in itself, and the context becomes the important consideration.

Claiming that those taken in verses 40 and 41 are taken away in the rapture, Gundry in discussing the parallel passage in Luke 17:34-37 ignores verse 37. There two are pictured in the same bed, with one taken and the other left. Two are grinding together, and one is taken and the other left. Two are in the field, one is taken and the other left. Then, in verse 37, the question is asked, "Where, Lord?" The answer is very dramatic: "And He said unto them, Wherever the body is, there will the eagles be gathered together." It should be very clear that the ones taken are put to death and their bodies are consumed by the vultures. If the ones taken are killed, then verses 40,41 of Matthew 24 speak of precisely the same kind of judgment as occurred in the flood where the ones taken were taken in judgment. Matthew 24 is just the reverse of the rapture, not the rapture itself.

The arguments of Gundry that one cannot harmonize this with the judgment of the nations is nonsensical. Before the Gentiles could be gathered in judgment, they obviously would have to be taken away as individuals. What is seen in Matthew 24:41,42 has its consummation in Matthew 25:31-46: they are parts of the same divine judgment that separates the saved from the unsaved at the beginning of the millennial kingdom.

These issues may be debated, but the most important point is that the translation of living saints, which is the main characteristic of the rapture, is found nowhere in Matthew. Only by assuming what he is trying to prove can a posttribulationist put the rapture in these passages.

It would be appropriate in a discussion of the doctrine of the rapture in the Gospels to consider the relationship of the sheep and the goats in Matthew 25:31-46. However, this will be discussed in relation to endtime events in chapter 11.

THE RAPTURE IN THE GOSPEL OF JOHN

While the synoptic Gospels frequently deal with the coming of Christ in relation to the Law of Moses and the future millennial kingdom, most expositors see in the Gospel of John a special character. As it was apparently the last of the four Gospels and written late in the first century, John presents from the sayings of Christ certain truths especially related to the church. Thus the Upper Room Discourse, the fourth and final great discourse of Christ, deals almost entirely with truth that anticipates the present age. It is natural to assume that here Christ would introduce the subject of the rapture.

This Jesus does in the familiar opening verses of John 14, where Christ stated, "In my Father's house are many mansions; if it were not so, I would have told you. I go to prepare a place for you. And if I go and prepare a place for you, I will come again, and receive you unto myself; that where I am, there you may be also" (vv. 2,3). Some expositors have viewed this as referring to the Christian's death and entrance into heaven, but many posttribulationists and pretribulationists recognize this as a reference to the rapture. J. Barton Payne is an exception to the normal conservative interpretation when he holds that John 14 refers to a believer's death.[9] Gundry therefore is correct when he replies, "Nothing is said concerning the death of believers generally."[10] Gundry's exegesis of the passage, however, leaves much to be desired.

The passage taken in its plain meaning says that Christ is going to leave the disciples and that they will not be able to follow Him. His purpose in leaving them is that He needs to prepare a place in the Father's house, an obvious reference to heaven, to which Christ is going to ascend. When He states that He is coming after them to receive them unto Himself so that they can be where He is, the implication is rather clear that He is taking them to the place He has prepared for them.

Gundry scoffs at the concept that the church will go to heaven for approximately seven years and return later with Christ to the millennial earth. Heaven is something more than a place: it is where Christ is. The church will be with Christ wherever He is, whether in heaven, the millennial earth, or the New Jerusalem. It is no more strange that the church will spend seven years in heaven in the Father's house than it is that the church will spend a thousand years on the millennial earth and then later spend eternity in the New Jerusalem.

Gundry attempts to substitute for the concept of heaven the idea that the disciples are already in the Father's house. He states, "In order to console the disciples concerning His going away, Jesus tells them that His leaving will work to their advantage. He is going to prepare for them *spiritual abodes within His own person.* Dwelling in these abiding places they will belong to God's household. This He will accomplish by going to the cross and then ascending to the Father. But He will return to receive the disciples into His immediate presence forever. Thus, the rapture will not have the purpose of taking them to heaven. It rather follows that from their being in Christ, in whom each believer already has an abode."[11]

One is at a loss to know how to comment on such fanciful exegesis. If the passage says anything, it says that Christ is going to leave the disciples to go to heaven, not simply leave them by dying. The Father's house is not on earth, and Christ is not going to remain in the earthly sphere in His bodily presence. The expression "I will come" must be spiritualized and deprived of its real meaning to allow Gundry's explanation. To spiritualize the Father's house and make it *"spiritual abodes within His own person"* is spiritualization to an extreme. The believer is unquestionably in Christ, but this is not the same as being in the Father's house.

It is most significant that Gundry, who claims to be a literalist when he deals with the first passage that clearly reveals the rapture, is forced to spiritualization in order to avoid the pretribulation rapture.

The extreme form of exegesis to which Gundry is driven in this passage is to escape the implication that the rapture is different from the second coming of Christ to set up His kingdom. In contrast to the description of the second coming in Matthew 24 — where important events, including the great tribulation, are seen to precede it — Christ gives in John 14 no preceding events, no signs, and the bare promise that they should be looking for His coming. This conflicts with the posttribulational view of the rapture and explains the unusual exegesis of Gundry.

Conclusion

Taking the testimony of the Gospels as a whole, we may conclude that the rapture is not found at all in Matthew, Mark, or

Luke, although the second coming of Christ is clearly spoken of and the events that precede it are described. In John 14 Christ introduces for the first time the subject of His coming for His own and His taking them to the Father's house.

The somewhat desperate attempt of posttribulationists to spiritualize this passage and eliminate it as referring to the rapture is in itself a confession that the rapture is presented in John 14 as an event distinctive from the second coming. That Christ did not expound the details of the rapture here is understandable, for the disciples had many other spiritual and theological problems at the time. The full explanation awaited the revelation which would be given through Paul and which formed a central theme of the epistles he wrote to the Thessalonians.

Emerging in Gundry's discussion of the rapture in the Gospels are the same problems which surface in other posttribulational approaches. Gundry does not apply the literal interpretation of prophecy in any consistent way, even though he claims to be a literalist, and it becomes very obvious that he is selecting only the facts that suit his argument, avoiding contradiction. This leads to an imperfect theological induction. When all the facts are taken into consideration, Gundry's conclusions are shown to be questionable.

Notes

[1] For a more complete statement on Matthew 13, see John F. Walvoord, *Matthew: Thy Kingdom Come* (Chicago: Moody Press, 1974), pp. 95-108.

[2] Robert H. Gundry, *The Church and the Tribulation* (Grand Rapids: Zondervan Publishing House, 1973), pp. 142-45.

[3] Ibid., pp. 143-44.

[4] Ibid., p. 129.

[5] Walvoord, *Matthew: Thy Kingdom Come*, pp. 179-204.

[6] Gundry, *The Church and the Tribulation*, p. 134.

[7] Ibid., pp. 134-39; Alexander Reese, *The Approaching Advent of Christ* (London: Marshall, Morgan & Scott, 1937), pp. 214-15.

[8] Reese, *The Approaching Advent of Christ*, p. 215.

[9] J. Barton Payne, *The Imminent Appearing of Christ* (Grand Rapids: Wm. B. Eerdmans Publishing Co., 1962), p. 74.

[10] Gundry, *The Church and the Tribulation*, p. 152, footnote.

[11] Ibid., p. 154 (italics in original).

Chapter 8

The Comforting Hope of
1 Thessalonians 4

Although the rapture of the church was introduced by Christ the night before His crucifixion, as recorded in John 14: 1-3, the details of the rapture were not revealed in Scripture until 1 Thessalonians was written. It is not too much to say that 1 Thessalonians 4–5 is probably the most important passage dealing with the rapture in the New Testament. Additional passages are 1 Corinthians 15:51-58 and 2 Thessalonians 2:1-12; but more detail is given in 1 Thessalonians 4 than in any other passage.

Probably more pretribulationists base their conclusion for a pretribulational rapture on 1 Thessalonians 4 than on any other single passage of Scripture. By contrast, evidence indicates that posttribulationists find little of a positive character to help them in the details of this revelation. It would seem natural, if the great tribulation actually intervened before the rapture could be fulfilled, that this would have been a good place to put the whole matter into proper perspective, as Christ did in Matthew 24 in His description of the events leading up to His second coming.

THE PROBLEM OF DEATH IN RELATION TO THE RAPTURE

We should bear in mind as we deal with this central passage on the rapture that the Thessalonian Christians had had only a few weeks of doctrinal instruction before Paul, Silas, and Timothy left them. It is amazing that their instruction included such doctrines as election (1:4), the Holy Spirit (1:5,6; 4:8; 5:19), conversion (1:9), assurance of salvation (1:5), sanctification (4:3; 5:23), and teachings on the Christian life. Obviously there were great gaps in their understanding of theology in general, and more particularly of the prophetic future events.

It is most significant that in every chapter in 1 Thessalonians some mention is made of the future coming of Christ. The Thessalonians are described as those who are "to wait for his Son from heaven" (1:10). They will be trophies of Paul's gospel ministry at the coming of the Lord (2:19), and their ultimate sanctification is promised when Christ comes (3:13).

Although 1 Thessalonians 4:13-18 is addressed to correct their ignorance about the rapture, it is quite clear that Paul is not introducing a new subject, but clarifying an old one. He had faithfully told them of the possibility of Christ's coming, and it was with this eager expectation that they were exhorted to wait for the rapture. It is implied that the thought had not occurred to them that some of them would die before the rapture. Accordingly, when some of their number, after such a brief time, had passed into the presence of the Lord through death, they were unprepared for it.

As many commentators have pointed out, it is possible that the hopelessness of the pagan world may have affected their hope in resurrection. Yet the certainty of resurrection to which Paul refers in 1 Thessalonians 4:14 is so inseparable from the gospel itself that it seems highly questionable that they had any real doubt whether their loved ones in Christ would be resurrected. Rather, their problem was how the future resurrection related to Christ's coming for the living saints. This was the problem Paul attacked and on which they needed further revelation.

As 1 Thessalonians 4:13-18 clearly shows, their fears were groundless. Their loved ones who had died would be resurrected, for all practical purposes, at the same time that the living would be raptured. They would, therefore, not have an inferior experience, and those living who were raptured would not have to wait for a period of time until their loved ones were resurrected.

POSTTRIBULATIONAL INTERPRETATION OF 1 THESSALONIANS 4

Posttribulationists usually do not treat 1 Thessalonians 4–5 extensively. Gundry is an exception and devotes a whole chapter to it.[1] Ladd discusses it for only a few pages, with references scattered throughout his discussion, at the same time devoting a third of his book to the historical argument for posttribulationism.[2]

In 1 Thessalonians 4, posttribulationists face a major difficulty. As presented here, the hope of the rapture is an imminent hope with no events such as the great tribulation regarded as intervening. Posttribulationists must find some explanation for this silence and for the major problem that the hope of the Lord's return is presented as a comfort to the Thessalonians sorrowing for their loved ones who have died. The hope of a rapture occurring after a literal great tribulation would be small comfort to those in this situation. Thus posttribulationists have marshalled a number of arguments in an attempt to answer both problems and others that face them in this passage.

Generally posttribulationists encounter the following problems in 1 Thessalonians 4: (1) the nature of this supposed delay of the resurrection of the dead in Christ; (2) the nature of the revelation claimed to have been received "by the word of the Lord"; (3) the meaning of the revelation that saints will meet the Lord in the air; (4) the problem of emphasis on translation as opposed to resurrection; (5) the problem of silence concerning any warning of the coming great tribulation; (6) the problem of the exhortation to comfort in view of the rapture of the church.

The nature of the supposed delay. The first problem faced by all expositors is discerning the reasons for the unusual sorrow of the Thessalonians over the death of their fellow believers. Various explanations have been given as to why they feared a delay in the resurrection of the dead in Christ that would place it after the rapture of the church. Pretribulationists have a convenient and plausible explanation in the possibility that the resurrection of the dead in Christ occurs at the end of the great tribulation when the tribulation martyrs will be raised (Rev. 20:4). Even Gundry mentions this: "We might think that the sorrow of the Thessalonians derived from the mistaken belief in a remaining behind of deceased believers at a pretribulational rapture with a consequent later date of resurrection, perhaps after the tribulation."[3] This would make sense if the Thessalonians had been taught pretribulationism.

In rejecting the pretribulational explanation of the possibility of delay in the resurrection of the dead in Christ, Gundry offers instead another interpretation. He writes, "The Thessalonians further thought that departed brethren, along with the wicked dead, will not rise until after the Messianic kingdom, and thus will miss the blessedness of Christ's earthly reign. This view gives a more substantial basis for the Thessalonians' sorrow than the notion that the dead in Christ will be left out of the pretribulational rapture."[4] It is curious that Gundry discards the pretribulational argument because it is based on an assumption, but considers as cogent and plausible the posttribulational argument also built on an assumption.

There are some real problems with Gundry's explanation. First, it is a new interpretation never before adopted by any other writer, whether pretribulational or posttribulational. Second, Gundry offers no factual support for his view. Third, pretribulationists can point to the fact that the Thessalonians had had some instruction on tribulation in general (cf. 1 Thess. 3:4), as well as the coming great tribulation specifically (2 Thess. 2:5-6). In other words, they had in mind the idea of a coming great tribulation which would be a time barrier between the rapture, if viewed as imminent, and the resurrection of the dead in Christ, which might occur after the great tribulation. Fourth, there is no indication anywhere in the Thessalonian epistles that their instruction included details of the millennium.

Gundry is grasping at a straw in injecting an explanation of the problem that has no support in the Scriptures. He undoubtedly does this only because he has no more plausible view to offer. While the Thessalonians might conceivably have had some grounds for confusion concerning the time of resurrection if they were pretribulational in outlook, why would they consider a delay necessary until after the millennium which was really not their immediate concern?

While both pretribulationists and posttribulationists can only speculate concerning the reason for the Thessalonians' concern, it seems the pretribulationists at least have some scriptural support for their view, whereas Gundry has none.

The nature of the revelation of the rapture "by the word of the Lord." Most scholars have little trouble with the expression "by the word of the Lord" (1 Thess. 4:15) by which Paul explains the source of his information about the rapture. Gundry seizes on this expression, however, to offer several explanations, including a rather fanciful proposal for the meaning of this term. He claims Paul may have gotten this from oral tradition of Jesus' teaching in the Olivet Discourse.[5] For this Gundry has to claim the existence of oral tradition transmitted so accurately that Paul would have before him these precise sayings of Jesus. This is extreme conjecture that has no support in any factual information in our possession and is especially contradicted by Galatians 1:15-19, in which Paul disavows transmission of information from the apostles to him. As Galatians was written about the same time or even later than 1 Thessalonians, it would make Paul's claim that he had not received transmitted information applicable to both epistles.

The purpose of Gundry's explanation is to avoid the idea that the rapture is a new revelation distinct from the second coming to the earth. One gets the impression that Gundry is unnecessarily belaboring a point which is actually not essential to his posttribulationism. It is much more plausible to hold, as most other posttribulationists do, that Paul received this truth as he did the gospel as a whole — by direct divine revelation. While the doctrine of Christ's coming is a truth clearly revealed in both the Old and New Testaments long before 1 Thessalonians was written, the concept of a translation of living saints going to heaven without dying was a new idea; even posttribulationists like Ladd have no trouble accepting this. It is rather surprising that Gundry will go to such lengths to prove a point that is actually irrelevant.

The question of why saints meet the Lord in the air. A crucial point in the revelation of 1 Thessalonians 4 is the truth that the saints at the time of the rapture will meet the Lord in the air. As this is the express statement of Scripture, both posttribulationists and pretribulationists must accept this revelation as valid. The question remains, however, why the saints meet the Lord in the air, and what will happen after this event.

Pretribulationists have an easy answer, because for them it is the fulfillment of John 14:1-3, in which Christ promised to come for His own and take them to the Father's house, which is considered equivalent to heaven. Gundry's spiritualization of the term "the Father's house" to get away from the idea that the saints go to heaven has been previously discussed and refuted (see chapter 7). Pretribulationists therefore view Christ's coming to the air above the earth as fulfillment of His purpose to receive His bride and take her back to heaven to the Father's house.

Posttribulationists have a twofold problem: (1) to explain why the church leaves the earth to meet the Lord in the air, and (2) to prove that the saints, having met the Lord in the air, change direction and proceed to the earth.

Gundry debates this as follows: "Other things being equal, the word 'descend' (*katabaino*) indicates a complete, uninterrupted descent, like that of the Spirit at Christ's baptism (Matt. 3:16; Mark 1:10; Luke 3:22; John 1:32,33) and that of Christ in His first advent (John 3:13; 6:33,38,41,42,50,51,58). Where a reversal from downward to upward motion comes into view, a specific statement to that effect appears, as in Acts 10:11,16 ('a certain object coming down, . . . and immediately the object was taken up into the sky'). In the absence of a statement indicating a halt or sudden reversal of direction, we naturally infer a complete descent to the earth, such as will take place only at the posttribulational advent."[6]

It should be noted that Gundry is attempting to solve this problem by definition of a word, a definition quite arbitrary and slanted in the direction of his conclusion. The text does declare that the church will meet the Lord in the air, which at least implies a halt for the meeting, even if it does not specify a change in direction. Gundry here again appeals to the argument from silence, which so often he disallows for the pretribulational view. He says, "But surely it is strange that in this, the fullest description of the rapture, there should be no mention of a change in direction from earthward to heaven, or of a halt. The absence of a specific phrase such as 'to the earth' cannot be very significant, for there is not one NT account of the second coming which contains such a phrase."[7] Here, on the one hand, Gundry argues from silence that there should be mention of a change in direction if such took place, but he discounts the silence of the passage on any indication of its continued direction to the earth.

Actually a meeting such as this does not necessarily indicate continued movement in the same direction. In Mark 14:13, the disciples were to meet the man bearing a pitcher and follow him. In Luke 17:12, which records the incident of the lepers' meeting Christ, He made no effort to accompany them back to where they came. Although the Greek words used here are different from those in 1 Thessalonians 4, the passage confirms the idea that to assume a meeting in the air requires Christ to continue to earth is reading into the passage what it does not say and does not require.

Most posttribulationists are silent on why the church rises from earth at all, though Gundry comments on this.[8] Why would it not be better for the saints to remain on earth when Christ returns and allow Him to separate them from the unsaved? This, in fact, is what pretribulationists believe occurs at the second coming of Christ to the earth, when the living Israelites are separated from other nations and gathered for judgment (Ezek. 20:34-38), and the sheep and the goats are gathered on earth to be separated (Matt. 25:31-46). Indeed, at the second coming of Christ, He will proceed directly to the earth without any interruption at all (see Rev. 19 and similar passages). His coming for the rapture, however, has a different purpose, namely, to take the church out of the earth.

From the pretribulational standpoint, therefore, it is plausible that the church should meet Him in the air. From the posttribulational standpoint, it is an unnecessary and an unlikely event. While neither posttribulationists nor pretribulationists can argue with finality from the text of 1 Thessalonians 4 on this point, it becomes obvious that the posttribulationists have more of a problem than the pretribulationists on the clearly stated meeting in the air. If the purpose of Christ is to take the church out of the earth to heaven, meeting Christ in the air would be natural. If the purpose of Christ is to come to the earth, it is not really necessary for the church to rise from earth into the air. Accordingly, for the posttribulationist to say that there is implication that Christ will come all the way to the earth at the rapture is an unsupported dogmatism.

The emphasis on translation as opposed to resurrection. In the interpretation of 1 Thessalonians 4, all agree Paul is explaining that the resurrection of the saints will occur at the same time as the translation of the living. The timing of the two events is a new revelation to the Thessalonians. However, as far as Scripture as a whole is concerned, the doctrine of resurrection is a familiar truth found in both the Old and New Testaments, whereas the idea of a translation of living saints is a new revelation. Thus the main point for Christians today is that 1 Thessalonians 4 presents in clear detail the fact that Christians living in the last generation will not die, but will meet the Lord and enter into their eternal relationship to Him without experiencing death.

In these facts, posttribulationism has a specific problem. Passages relating to the second coming of Christ to the earth, such as Revelation 20:4, speak of resurrection *after* the arrival on earth at the time Christ enters His kingdom, not *during* the descent from heaven. The resurrection, however, is specified as relating to the martyred dead of those in the immediately preceding generation who had refused to worship the world ruler and consequently died for their faith. There is no indication in this text that the resurrection extends to any other class of people, such as the church as a whole.

In a similar way, Daniel 12:2 refers to a resurrection occurring after the tribulation mentioned in Daniel 12:1. This seems to refer to Old Testament saints, or at least to include them. In none of the passages in the Old or New Testaments where a resurrection is tied to the second coming of Christ to the earth is there any clear identification that the church is included. From the standpoint of pretribulational interpretation, this is no accident, but a clear revelation that all people are not raised at the same time. Revelation 20, of course, also distinguishes the resurrection mentioned in verse 4 from the resurrection of the wicked which occurs after the millennium (v. 12), as is usually understood by premillenarians.

Posttribulationists usually argue that the resurrection of Revelation 20:4-6 is declared to be "the first resurrection." On the basis that it is called "the first resurrection," they argue that no resurrection can precede it, such as a rapture at the beginning of the tribulation. Ladd argues along this line and asks the question, "Does the Word similarly teach that the first resurrection will consist of two stages, the first of which will occur at the beginning of the Tribulation? No such teaching appears in Scripture."9

The problem here is the common misunderstanding of what the word *first* means. *First* does not mean the number one resurrection, but rather that the resurrection here revealed occurs before the final resurrection in the millennium, mentioned in Revelation 20:12-14. It merely means that the resurrection occurs first or *before* the later resurrection.

Indeed, everyone has to agree that the resurrection of Jesus Christ Himself is the first resurrection. Any subsequent resurrection could not be resurrection number one. Also, in Matthew 27:52,53 a token resurrection of some saints occurred in Jerusalem at the time of Christ's resurrection. The resurrection of Christ and these saints is the token of the resurrections to come. Accordingly, if there can be two separate resurrections which are already history, why should it be thought incredible that there should be more than one resurrection of the righteous still to be fulfilled, namely, the resurrection of the church or the saints of the present age before the tribulation, and the resurrection of the Old Testament saints and the tribulation saints who die just before the time of Christ's coming to set up His kingdom? Logically, no argument can be built for posttribulationism on the word *first* because all these resurrections are "first," or before the final resurrection of the wicked at the end of the millennium.

The real embarrassment of the posttribulationists, however, is that not a single passage related to the resurrection at the time of Christ's second coming to the earth has anything at all to say about a translation of any saints, much less a specific translation for the church living on the earth. Most pretribulationists insist that there is no translation at all at the end of the tribulation; instead, the saints then living on earth enter the millennial kingdom in their natural bodies, not translated bodies. In view of the many passages that deal with both the subject of resurrection and the second coming of Christ to the earth, it is certainly a strange silence that there should be no clear passage indicating that any of the saints living on earth at that time should be translated. The alleged translation of the saints in Matthew 24:40,42 has already been demonstrated to be no rapture at all, but a taking away in judgment.

Therefore the emphasis on translation in 1 Thessalonians 4 and in other passages such as 1 Corinthians 15:51-52, which have no clear contextual relationship to a second coming to the earth, leaves the posttribulationists groping for any proof that the rapture occurs at the end of the tribulation. Their frequently asserted accusation against the pretribulationists — that pretribulationism is based on inference — is a hollow charge when it must follow that posttribulationism is also built on an inference. The fact that a translation is necessary to the resurrection of 1 Thessalonians 4 sets this apart as different from any other resurrection mentioned in the Bible which includes no translation of living saints.

Lack of warning of great tribulation. The rapture passages are distinguished by there being no warning of an impending great tribulation. In every instance where the rapture is clearly intended as the meaning, there is an absence of impending events; in contrast to revelations concerning the second coming of Christ, such as Matthew 24 or Revelation 4-18. If they are at all comprehensive, they uniformly mention events that precede and serve as signs of the approaching second coming. By contrast, these signs are lacking in all the major rapture passages.

This is especially pointed out in 1 Thessalonians 4, where the truth of the rapture is presented in considerable detail. No word of caution is given contextually that they should not look for this event until other events occur first — quite in contrast to the revelation concerning the second coming to the earth. Posttribulationists have no real answer to this problem, and they tend to ignore it.

The exhortation to comfort. Undoubtedly the greatest problem posttribulationists face in 1 Thessalonians 4 is that the doctrine of the rapture is offered as a comfort to those who have lost loved ones in Christ through death. It is certainly a hollow argument to say that the truth presented is that of their resurrection. There seems to be no serious question that the Thessalonians believed in the doctrine of resurrection. They did have questions as to where this occurred in the prophetic scheme. This was primarily because the hope of the Lord's return for living Christians had been taught to them as an imminent hope, and they were actually waiting momentarily for His return.

If, as Gundry and Ladd agree, the great tribulation will be a time of great suffering and trial with many martyrs, and a Christian who enters this period must somehow survive the edict that all nonworshipers of the beast be put to death before he can hope to be raptured as a living saint, then the expectation of survival through such an awful period of suffering is small comfort. It would mean first that they could not possibly see their loved ones for years to come. It would mean that in the path ahead lay extreme suffering and privation and probably martyrdom. How, under these circumstances, could they derive any comfort from such a sequence of events? It would be far better from their point of view if the tribulation were to be indefinitely postponed and they were to live out normal lives and die and await resurrection at the rapture. The prospects would certainly be preferable to the possibility of survival through the great tribulation.

Though not totally ignoring this point, posttribulationists have still to explain how the Thessalonians could derive any comfort whatever out of a posttribulational rapture, and how this would add at all to their faith and expectation at the time that they had lost loved ones through death. Those who, like J. Barton Payne, deny a literal, seven-year tribulation and therefore have a concept of genuine imminency of the Lord's return can with some justification offer comfort to Christians whose loved ones have died. But others, like Ladd and Gundry, who agree to a literal seven-year tribulation offer a most unconvincing solution by simply saying that the ultimate hope of resurrection is all that is in view. If the only way a Christian can experience the rapture is to survive the tribulation, it is no longer either a comforting hope or a blessed hope. Instead there should be grim preparation for probable martyrdom in the most awful time of human suffering and persecution of which Scripture speaks.

Gundry posits several arguments to solve this difficulty in posttribulationism. In general, he first tries to soften the rigors of the tribulation by making it a time of satanic wrath instead of divine wrath. This has been previously discussed (see chapter 6). Actually, if his view of the tribulation is right, it works against what he is trying to prove, because Satan's wrath is specifically against Christian believers and Israel. If Gundry is right, it emphasizes the rigors of the tribulation, instead of softening them. Any reasonably literal interpretation of the Book of Revelation, such as Ladd and Gundry attempt, should make clear that probably the majority of believers who are in the great tribulation will perish. The percentage of Jews who perish in the land is said to be two-thirds (Zech. 13:8). The world's population as a whole will probably be reduced to less than half (Rev. 6:8; 9:15). Such a prospect is hardly harmonious with a message of comfort. Only an imminent translation could provide real comfort.

Even posttribulationists like Ladd recognize that the translation of the living saints is the most important truth. Ladd writes, "God had never before revealed to men what would be the particular lot of the living saints at the end of the age. The doctrine of the resurrection had long been taught (cf. Dn. 12:2), but the fact that the living are to put on the resurrection bodies at the moment of the Lord's return without passing through death and join the resurrected dead in the presence of Christ is revealed for the first time through the Apostle Paul."[10]

Generally, posttribulationists tend to ignore the problem of how a posttribulational rapture could be a comfort. They dogmatically deny that comfort is affected by the prospect of the great tribulation. Gundry, for instance, attempts to dispose of the problem in two paragraphs.[11] Such a feeble attempt to erase the problem is an obvious confession that he has no realistic solution to offer. The prospect of the rapture after the tribulation is small comfort to those facing martyrdom. It is not too much to say that this is a most difficult problem to posttribulationists; as a group they tend to evade it rather than face up to it.

If a delay in the resurrection of the dead in Christ were a concern to the Thessalonian believers, how much more would have been their concern if they faced the prospect of dying as martyrs and joining these dead in Christ? Further, if martyrdom were a probability, they should have rejoiced that the dead in Christ had escaped the rigors of the tribulation. According to Revelation 14:13, the voice from heaven declares those who die as "blessed" because they will escape the persecution of believers in the great tribulation. As Hiebert expresses it, "But if they had been taught that the church must go through the great tribulation the logical reaction for them would have been to rejoice that these loved ones had escaped that great period of suffering which they felt was about to occur."[12]

Posttribulationists by and large do not solve their problems in 1 Thessalonians 4. The expectation of the Lord's return is uniformly pictured as an imminent event. Their prospect for imminent rapture was such that they feared a delay in resurrection for the dead in Christ. Posttribulationists have no adequate explanation for Paul's omission of any warning that the great tribulation was ahead and necessarily preceded the rapture; under the circumstances, such an omission would have been most misleading and contrasts sharply with the clear presentation of events leading up to the second coming of Christ recorded in Matthew 24.

SUMMARY OF POSTTRIBULATIONAL INTERPRETATION OF 1 THESSALONIANS 4

As a whole, the posttribulationists' interpretation of 1 Thessalonians 4 does little to advance their argument. They have no reasonable explanation how a posttribulational rapture offers comfort to sorrowing Thessalonians. They have no satisfactory answer why Paul is silent on the impending great tribulation. There is no good explanation why the rapture is portrayed as an impending event. There is no reasonable connection between this passage and the Olivet Discourse. The rapture of living saints is a new revelation not connected with the second coming of Christ in previous revelations, as even posttribulationists like Ladd concede.

Obviously posttribulationism is at its weakest point in 1 Thessalonians 4, where the doctrine of the rapture has its most detailed revelation.

As the discourse relative to the future continues in 1 Thessalonians 5, however, posttribulationists have posed some problems for pretribulationists that warrant careful attention. These problems are considered next.

Notes

[1] Robert H. Gundry, *The Church and the Tribulation* (Grand Rapids: Zondervan Publishing House, 1973), pp. 100-111.

[2] George E. Ladd, *The Blessed Hope* (Grand Rapids: Wm. B. Eerdmans Publishing Co., 1956), pp. 77-80.

[3] Gundry, *The Church and the Tribulation*, p. 100.

[4] Ibid., p. 101.

[5] Ibid., p. 102.

[6] Ibid., p. 103.

[7] Ibid., p. 104.

[8] Ibid.

[9] Ladd, *The Blessed Hope*, p. 82.

[10] Ibid., p. 80.

[11] Gundry, *The Church and the Tribulation*, pp. 101-2.

[12] D. Edmond Hiebert, *The Thessalonian Epistles* (Chicago: Moody Press, 1971), p. 205.

Chapter 9

The Rapture and the Day of the Lord in 1 Thessalonians 5

The relationship of 1 Thessalonians 5 to the rapture has been debated by both pretribulationists and posttribulationists with an amazing variety of opinions. The problem centers in the definition of "the day of the Lord" and its relationship to the rapture. Because there are differences of interpretation among both pretribulationists and posttribulationists, generalizations are inadvisable. The center of the problem is, first of all, the question of what "the day of the Lord" means. A second question is why the day of the Lord is introduced immediately after discussion of the rapture. A third question is the meaning of specific statements relating to the time of the rapture.

THE MEANING OF THE DAY OF THE LORD

References to the day of the Lord abound in the Old Testament and occur occasionally in the New. Virtually everyone agrees that the judgments related to the second coming are in some sense a part of the day of the Lord. Definitions of the word *day* vary from a specific event, such as a twenty-four-hour day, to an extended period of time stretching all the way from the rapture to the end of the thousand-year reign of Christ. Generally speaking, pretribulationists have identified the day of the Lord as the millennial kingdom, including the judgments that introduce the kingdom. This view was popularized by the 1917 edition of the Scofield Reference Bible.[1] In this interpretation, for all practical purposes, the day of the Lord begins at the end of or after the great tribulation.

Pretribulationists who see the day of the Lord beginning at the end of the tribulation have difficulty harmonizing this with the pretribulational rapture. Posttribulationists point out that 1 Thessalonians 5, referring to the day of the Lord, immediately follows chapter 4, which reveals the rapture. As chapter 5 is dealing with the beginning of the day of the Lord, the implication is that the rapture and the beginning of the day of the Lord occur at the same time. Capitalizing on the confusion among pretribulationists in defining the day of the Lord, Alexander Reese spends a chapter of his classic work on posttribulationism, making the most of this argument.[2]

Reese holds that the use of the expression "the day" indicates that endtime events all occur in rapid succession, including the translation of the church and the various judgments of the saints and the wicked. He identifies the day of the Lord in 1 Thessalonians 5 with other references to "the day" as found in 1 Corinthians 3:13 and Romans 13:11,12. He likewise so identifies the expressions "in that day" (2 Thess. 1:10; 2 Tim. 1:18; 4:8); "the day of Christ" (Phil. 1:6,10; 2:16); "the day of the Lord Jesus Christ" (1 Cor. 1:7,8; 2 Cor. 1:14); and "the day of the Lord" (1 Cor. 5:4,5; 2 Thess. 2:1-3). According to Reese, all refer to the same time and the same event.

Reese and other posttribulationists, as their argument unfolds, lump together all references to "the day," ignoring the context, arguing in a circle, assuming that posttribulationism is true. As is frequently the case with difficult points of exegesis, it is of utmost importance that the context of each passage be considered before terms can be equated with similar wording elsewhere. Reese pays little attention to the variety of contextual backgrounds.

The central problem, however, is that this kind of explanation assumes that "the day" is a simple and uncomplicated reference to a point in time, whereas in fact the total view of Scripture indicates something quite different.

The subject of the day of the Lord is so extensive that a complete exposition would require a major work and would involve many references in both the Old and New Testaments. Nevertheless the matter can be simplified if truth relating to the day of the Lord is placed into three categories: (1) references to a day of the Lord as referring to any period of time in the past or future when God deals directly in judgment on human sin; (2) a day of the Lord in the sense of certain specific future events constituting a judgment of God; (3) the broadest possible sense of the term, indicating a time in which God deals directly with the human situation, both in judgment and in blessing, hence broad enough to include not only the judgments preceding the millennium but also the blessings of the millennium itself.

As we encounter the difficult problem of 1 Thessalonians 5, the broadest definition of the day of the Lord is indicated. This contrasts, for instance, with the use of the same term in 2 Thessalonians 2, where the narrower definition of the second category is illustrated. As this classification is not recognized by most posttribulationists and some pretribulationists, careful attention should be paid to every indication in 1 Thessalonians 5 as to the nature of the day of the Lord.

As many references to the day of the Lord make clear, the period involved is not a twenty-four-hour day, but rather an extended period of time — although the symbolism of a twenty-four-hour day is in view. Significantly the article *the* is not found in 1 Thessalonians 5, and therefore the phrase could be translated "*a* day of the Lord."

References to the day of the Lord, not actually a literal day, have in mind the symbolism of a day beginning at midnight and extending through twenty-four hours to the next midnight.

In this symbolism, the following points can be noted: (1) the day of the Lord indicates that the preceding day has ended as a time period, and a new time period has begun; (2) an ordinary day is usually a period of time which, at its beginning, is without major events — that is, people normally sleep from midnight until daybreak; (3) with the coming of the daylight, or after the time period is somewhat advanced, major events begin as the program for the day unfolds — as in a sense the day "comes to life" with daylight rather than at midnight; (4) as the morning hours of the day unfold, the major activities of the day take place, climaxing in the events of the evening hours; (5) as a twenty-four-hour day ends at midnight, so a new day follows with a new series of events.

If the symbolism of a twenty-four-hour day is followed, the various facts revealed in Scriptures relating to the day of the Lord begin to take on meaning and relationship. In its broadest dimension, the day of the Lord follows the present day of grace in which God is fulfilling both His work of salvation by grace and His rule of life by grace; God is not attempting to deal directly in any major way with human sin. Hence the rapture could well be the end of the day of grace and the beginning of the day of the Lord. The day of grace, all agree, is followed by a period in which God does deal directly with human sin in a series of judgments continuing into the millennial kingdom, which will be also a period in which God deals directly with human sin. All agree also that after the millennium, the eternal state begins, which is another "day" that some believe is designated as "the day of God" (2 Peter 3:12), the eternal day.

Before determining the significance of 1 Thessalonians 5 in relation to eschatology as a whole, it is necessary to establish firmly exactly what the day of the Lord is, as it is variously described in the Bible. It is strange that so many expositions of 1 Thessalonians 5 do not establish a definition of the day of the Lord and do not take into consideration the specific facts furnished in the Old Testament as well as in the New.

THE OLD TESTAMENT DOCTRINE OF THE DAY OF THE LORD

A study of numerous Old Testament references to the day of the Lord and "the day," as it is sometimes called, should make clear to anyone who respects the details of prophecy that the designation denotes an extensive time of divine judgment on the world. Among the texts are Isaiah 2:12-21; 13:9-16; 34:1-8; Joel 1:15–2:11, 28-32; 3:9-12; Amos 5:18-20; Obadiah 15-17; Zephaniah 1:7-18.

Examination of these references indicates, for example, that Isaiah 2 predicts divine judgment will fall on the wicked. The passage could be applied to the Old Testament captivity, now past, or it could be applied to a future time in connection with the second coming of Christ. The main characteristic of the day of the Lord brought out in this passage is judgment on man who has been living in rebellion against God. It is clear that the judgment is more than a single twenty-four-hour day, and is rather an extended period of divine judgment. It is a day of the Lord.

The dramatic picture of Isaiah 13:9-16, followed immediately by predictions concerning the destruction of Babylon by the Medes and the Persians, again gives graphic detail to the characteristics of the day of the Lord. It is described as "a destruction from the Almighty" (13:6). According to verse 9, "the day of the LORD cometh, cruel both with wrath and fierce anger, to lay the land desolate: and he shall destroy the sinners thereof out of it." Next Isaiah describes the stars and sun as being darkened, a prophecy that will be literally fulfilled in the great tribulation. In Isaiah 13:11, he states, "And I will punish the world for their evil, and the wicked for their iniquity; and I will cause the arrogancy of the proud to cease, and will lay low the haughtiness of the terrible."

Beginning with verse 17, Isaiah describes the Medes as destroying Babylon. In one sense this has already been fulfilled. In another sense this will not have a complete fulfillment until the time of the great tribulation. It is this mingled picture of judgment, regardless of when it occurs, that characterizes the day of the Lord. Any period of extensive divine judgment in the Old Testament is therefore "a day of the Lord." All of them will be eclipsed, however, with the final judgment that culminates in the great tribulation and the battle of the great day of God Almighty at the second coming of Christ.

The other references cited contain similar material. Isaiah 34:1-8 seems to indicate that judgments will fall on the world in the events leading up to the second coming.

Probably the most graphic picture is found in the Book of Joel, most of which is dedicated to describing the day of the Lord. Included is the famous prophecy of the outpouring of the Spirit, quoted in Acts 2:17-21, which occurred on the day of Pentecost but will have its complete fulfillment in the days prior to the second coming of Christ. The judgments of God poured out on the earth, as well as disturbances in heaven, are graphically described by Joel. There will be great signs in the heavens (Joel 2:30,31), described in more detail in the Book of Revelation: "And I will shew wonders in the heavens and in the earth, blood, and fire, and pillars of smoke. The sun shall be turned into darkness, and the moon into blood, before the great and terrible day of the LORD come." What is meant here is not that the day of the Lord will begin after these wonders in heaven, but that it will come to its climax when the judgment is actually executed.

The Book of Zephaniah adds another aspect to the day of the Lord. After revealing in some detail the judgments to occur at that time, the prophet describes the blessings that will follow (1:7-18). In Zephaniah 3:14-17 the prophet writes, "Sing, O daughter of Zion; shout, O Israel; be glad and rejoice with all the heart, O daughter of Jerusalem. The LORD hath taken away thy judgments, he hath cast out thine enemy: the king of Israel, even the LORD, is in the midst of thee: thou shalt not see evil any more. In that day it shall be said to Jerusalem, Fear thou not: and to Zion, Let not thine hands be slack. The LORD thy God in the midst of thee is mighty; he will save, he will rejoice over thee with joy; he will rest in his love, he will joy over thee with singing." The significant truth revealed here is that the day of the Lord which first inflicts terrible judgments ends with an extended period of blessing on Israel, which will be fulfilled in the millennial kingdom.

Based on the Old Testament revelation, the day of the Lord is a time of judgment, culminating in the second coming of Christ, and followed by a time of special divine blessing to be fulfilled in the millennial kingdom.

POSTTRIBULATIONAL INTERPRETATION OF THE DAY OF THE LORD

Generally posttribulationists like Reese and Gundry begin the day of the Lord at the end of the great tribulation. Gundry, who devotes a whole chapter to this, defines the day of the Lord in these words: "The 'day of the Lord,' with its corollary the 'day of Christ,' figures prominently in discussion of the rapture. In these phrases the term 'day' does not refer to twenty-four hours, but to a longer period of time, a period which includes the millennium and the final judgment. With reference to the time of the rapture, the crux of the argument lies in the *terminus a quo*, the beginning point, of the day of the Lord, not in its millennial extension."³

In his discussion he attempts to refute the idea that the day of the Lord begins earlier than the end of the tribulation. His discussion is somewhat difficult to follow, but in general he tries to refute all the contentions that the day of the Lord begins before the end of the great tribulation.

All agree that the climax of the day of the Lord, as far as judgment on the nations is concerned, comes at Armageddon and is furthered by the destruction of the armies at the second coming in Revelation 19. Many believe it is brought to its climax in the judgment of the nations after the second coming, as recorded in Matthew 25:31-46. The question remains whether this is all that is involved in the judgments.

Even a casual reading of the Book of Revelation will soon disclose that the divine judgments of God do not begin at the end of the tribulation, but certainly include the entire period of the tribulation itself. While Gundry attempts to rearrange the Book of Revelation so that the major judgments fall at its close, it is quite clear, for instance, that the fourth seal described in Revelation 6:7,8 — where one-fourth of the earth's population is destroyed — is not at the end, but in the earlier phase of the great tribulation. Certainly the destruction of one-fourth of the population would qualify as a day of the Lord for the earth.

The sixth seal describes in vivid detail the very things the Old Testament attributes to the day of the Lord. It states, "And I beheld, when he opened the sixth seal, and, lo, there was a great earthquake; and the sun became black as sackcloth of hair, and the moon became as blood; And the stars of the heaven fell unto the earth, even as a fig tree casteth her untimely figs, when she is shaken of a mighty wind. And the heaven departed as a scroll when it is rolled together; and every mountain and island were moved out of their places" (Rev. 6:12-14). This can be compared to Joel 2:30,31, as well as Joel 2:10,11. Unless the seals are twisted out of chronological sequence, this is not the end of the great tribulation; rather the great tribulation is in progress.

Gundry attempts to make all the catastrophic judgments of

the seals, trumpets, and vials as if they were in some way simultaneous. The very order of events described in the seven trumpets, however, as well as in the seven vials, indicates that there is chronological sequence and that all these judgments cannot be thrown together. The implication is clear that the great judgments of the day of the Lord extend over the entire great tribulation, even though all agree that they climax at its end, as God disposes in final judgments of the nations.

Gundry's motive in placing the day of the Lord at the extreme end of the tribulation is to get the church raptured before major events of the day of the Lord take place. In effect, he is trying to achieve a pre-day-of-the-Lord rapture, with the great judgments at Armageddon occurring immediately afterward. If Gundry is wrong in limiting the day of the Lord to the extreme end of the great tribulation, however, his view of posttribulation rapture means that the church will go through most of the terrible judgments, even if they were raptured just before the climax. Gundry's posttribulationism is built on a faulty concept of the day of the Lord not supported by the Scriptures that define what occurs in that period.

WHY IS THE DAY OF THE LORD INTRODUCED IN 1 THESSALONIANS 5?

In the debate between pretribulationism and posttribulationism, the question arises why the day of the Lord is introduced immediately after discussion of the rapture of the church. The fact that the rapture is mentioned first in chapter 4 before the day of the Lord is presented in chapter 5 is significant. The important subject was the rapture, including the resurrection of the dead in Christ and the translation of living believers. The rapture is not introduced as a phase of the day of the Lord and seems to be distinguished from it.

First Thessalonians 5 begins with the Greek particle *de*, which is normally used to introduce a new subject. It is found, for instance, when the rapture was introduced in 1 Thessalonians 4:13. Accordingly, it is clear that 1 Thessalonians 5 is not talking specifically about the rapture, but about another truth. The introduction of this material at this point, however, implies that it has some relationship to the preceding context. Accordingly, while it is not talking specifically about the rapture, it is dealing with the general subject of eschatology, of which the rapture is a part. Thus it would be a fair judgment that, to some extent, Paul is continuing his discussion by dealing with the broad program of endtime events as defined by the term "the day of the Lord."

For this reason D. Edmond Hiebert introduces his exegesis of 1 Thessalonians 5 with these words: "This paragraph is an appropriate companion piece to the preceding. It is the second half of the distinctively eschatological block of material in the epistle. The former offered needed instruction concerning the dead in Christ; this gives a word of needed exhortation to the living."[4]

The subject of chapter 5 is introduced with the statement, "But of the times and seasons, brethren, ye have no need that I write unto you." In contrast to instruction on the rapture, by which he was correcting their ignorance, Paul here states that he does not need to instruct them concerning "the times" (*chronoi*) and "the seasons" (*kairoi*). Though these terms are sometimes used interchangeably and both relate to time, the first seems to indicate duration, and the second the character or nature of the times. The New International Version uses the words "times and dates," with both plural.

In a word, Paul is saying that eschatological events involve a series of periods and events, of which the rapture is one, as he has already told the Thessalonians, and that specifically these events relate to the day of the Lord as a time period with special characteristics. In verse 2 he declares, "For yourselves know perfectly that the day of the Lord so cometh as a thief in the night." Much has been said about this figure of speech, and Paul expresses that they already knew what he meant by it. Obviously he is saying that they knew that the day of the Lord was certainly coming but, like a thief in the night, there was no way to date it.

In Paul's discussion that follows, a sharp contrast is drawn between the day of the Lord as it relates to the unsaved and as it relates to Christians. This is brought out in the use of the first and second persons — "we," "us," and "you" (vv. 1,2,4-6,8-11) — and the third person "they" and "others" (vv. 3,6,7). In verse 3 the day of the Lord is pictured as coming upon the unbelievers like travail upon a woman with child, so that they cannot escape, just as a woman cannot escape birth pangs. Paul further states that their destruction will come at a time when they are saying "peace and safety." Gundry does not explain why they will be saying "peace and safety" toward the end of the great tribulation, as it does not fit into his view. Payne has no problem with this and regards it as a sense of false security that exists today in spite of atomic bombs and the danger of a holocaust.[5]

The idea that the expression "saying peace and safety" refers to the longing for peace and safety on the part of those who are in the great tribulation is not an acceptable explanation and is rejected by both posttribulationists and pretribulationists. The fact is that Gundry is faced with a real problem of trying to fit this into his scheme with the day of the Lord beginning toward the end of the great tribulation. First Thessalonians 5 states that people will be saying "peace and safety" before the great tribulation begins. This is in harmony with pretribulationism, but quite out of harmony with posttribulationism.

Paul states that the day of the Lord will not overtake the Thessalonians as a thief. Why does an event coming as a thief come unexpectedly upon the world, but with proper expectation for believers? Paul explains this in verses 4 and 5: "But you, brothers, are not in darkness so that this day should surprise you like a thief. You are all sons of the light and sons of the day. We do not belong to the night or to the darkness" (NIV). Here is a crucial point in Paul's explanation: the thief is going to come in the night, but the believers are declared not to belong to the night or the darkness. The implication is quite clear that believers are in a different time reference, namely, that they belong to the day that precedes the darkness.

On this basis Paul gives an exhortation. If the Thessalonians are of the day, they are not to be asleep or drugged; rather they are to be sober or self-controlled, "putting on faith and love as a breastplate, and the hope of salvation as a helmet" (v. 8 NIV). Paul concludes in verse 9, "For God did not appoint us to suffer wrath, but to receive salvation through our Lord Jesus Christ" (NIV).

In the exegesis of this verse, pretribulationists and post-tribulationists part company. Posttribulationists insist that the

church is not appointed to wrath, and with this all pretribulationists agree. What the passage is talking about, however,
is not wrath in the abstract, but a *time* of wrath. The judgments
poured out in the tribulation do not single out unsaved people
only, for war, pestilence, famine, earthquakes, and stars falling
from heaven afflict the entire population except for the 144,000 of
Revelation 7 singled out by God for special protection.

Here, however, the believer in Christ is assured that his
appointment is not to this time of wrath. In attempting to explain
this, the pretribulationist has the obvious advantage: if the church
is raptured before this time of trouble, then all that is said in this
passage becomes very clear; that is, the period of wrath will not
overtake the church as a thief, because the church will not be
there. If Gundry's use of the argument from silence is valid, it
would seem here that Paul's silence on the matter of whether the
church must endure this period is again another indication that
the church will not even enter the period.

When we take the total picture of this passage into consideration, the reason for Paul's introducing it becomes clearer. Although the events of the day of the Lord do not begin immediately
after the rapture, the time period as such — following the symbolism of a day beginning at midnight — could easily be understood to begin with the rapture itself. The opening hours of the day
of the Lord do not contain great events. Gradually the major
events of the day of the Lord unfold, climaxing in the terrible
judgments with which the great tribulation is brought to conclusion.

Taken as a whole, the pretribulational point of view gives
sense and meaning to 1 Thessalonians 5 and explains why this is
introduced after the rapture. In effect, Paul is saying that the time
of the rapture cannot be determined any more than the time of the
beginning of the day of the Lord, but this is of no concern to
believers because our appointment is not the wrath of the day of
the Lord, but rather the salvation which is ours in Christ.

Confirmation is given to this approach to 1 Thessalonians 5
in a study of 2 Thessalonians 2, where the day of the Lord is again
introduced, this time in a context in which the Thessalonians
misunderstood and needed correction.

A further word needs to be said concerning the relationship of the day of the Lord to "the day of Christ." Gundry argues at length that the various forms of the six occurrences of this phrase (1 Cor. 1:8; 5:5; 2 Cor. 1:14; Phil. 1:6,10; 2:16) do not justify any distinction from the basic term "the day of the Lord." This is an exegetical problem that does not really affect the question of pretribulationism and posttribulationism. The contexts of these passages are taken by many to refer to the rapture as a specific event in contrast to the day of the Lord as an extended period of time. If the context of each passage, along with all the references to "the day," is taken into consideration, there is really no problem. Even if Gundry is right in holding that these passages refer to the day of the Lord, they can be understood to refer to the beginning of the extended period of time which follows. It is again begging the question to assume this teaches posttribulationism, and Gundry does.

Gundry summarizes his viewpoint in a way that misrepresents the pretribulational position. He states, "In the NT sixteen expressions appear in which the term 'day' is used eschatologically. Twenty times 'day' appears without a qualifying phrase. In view of the wide variety of expressions and the numerous instances where 'day' occurs without special qualification, it seems a very dubious procedure to select five out of the sixteen expressions, lump together four of the five as equivalent to one another, and distinguish the four from the one remaining. There is no solid basis, then, for distinguishing between the day of Christ and the day of the Lord."[6]

The reference in 1 Corinthians 5:5 has a textual problem, and some texts read "the day of the Lord." Pretribulationists are justified in distinguishing the remaining five texts from the day of the Lord because the expression "the day of the Lord" is not expressly used. Pretribulationists do not claim that this proves the pretribulation rapture; what they point to is that if the pretribulational rapture is established on other grounds, these references seem to refer specifically to the rapture rather than to the time of judgment on the world. This is based on what each passage states. It is, therefore, manifestly unfair to accuse pretribulationists of arbitrarily lumping things together that have no distinguishing characteristics. On the contrary, the posttribulationist is lumping together a number of different phrases that are not quite the same without any regard for the context or their precise wording.

Alexander Reese proceeds much on the same basis as Gundry when he declares that all references to "the day" refer to the day of the Lord.[7] He does this without any supporting evidence. Yet the word *day* occurs more than two hundred times in the New Testament alone and only becomes an eschatological term when the context so indicates. The only way all these eschatological terms can be made to refer specifically to the day of the Lord is to assume that posttribulationism is true and argue from this premise. Pretribulationists rightfully object to this illogical procedure.

Taken as a whole, 1 Thessalonians 5 — while not in itself a conclusive argument for pretribulationism — is more easily harmonized with the pretribulational interpretation than the posttribulational interpretation. The passage is quite strange as an explanation of the time of the rapture if, in fact, the Thessalonians were taught posttribulationism and already knew that they would have to go through the day of the Lord. The beginning of the day of the Lord under those circumstances would have no relationship to the rapture and would be no comfort to them in their sorrow. On the other hand, if the rapture occurs before the endtime tribulation and the day of the Lord begins at the time of the pretribulation rapture, then the discussion is cogent because the indeterminant character of the beginning of the day of the Lord is the same as the indeterminant time of the rapture itself.

Nowhere in 1 Thessalonians 4 or 5 is the rapture specifically placed after the great tribulation and as occurring at the time of the climax of the judgments which are brought on the world at the time of the day of the Lord. On the contrary, the Thessalonians are assured that their appointment is not a day of wrath, but a day of salvation, a concept easily harmonized with the pretribulational interpretation.

Notes

[1] Scofield Reference Bible, Note, p. 1272.

[2] Alexander Reese, *The Approaching Advent of Christ* (London: Marshall, Morgan & Scott, 1937), pp. 17-83. Cf. discussion by John F. Walvoord, *The Rapture Question* (Findlay, Ohio: Dunham Publishing Co., 1957), pp. 161-72.

[3] Robert H. Gundry, *The Church and the Tribulation* (Grand Rapids: Zondervan Publishing House, 1973), p. 89.

[4] D. Edmond Hiebert, *The Thessalonian Epistles* (Chicago: Moody Press), p. 207.

[5] J. Barton Payne, *The Imminent Appearing of Christ* (Grand Rapids: Wm. B. Eerdmans Publishing Co., 1962), p. 108.

[6] Gundry, *The Church and the Tribulation*, p. 98.

[7] Reese, *The Approaching Advent of Christ*, pp. 167-83.

Chapter 10

Is the Tribulation Before the Rapture in 2 Thessalonians?

Posttribulationists often cite two passages in 2 Thessalonians in support of their viewpoint. The first concerns the comfort extended to the Thessalonians in their persecution in 1:5-10; the second is the word of correction concerning Paul's teaching which had reached the Thessalonians, as stated in 2:1-12. A third reference — 2 Thessalonians 3:5, where the believers are exhorted to "patient waiting for Christ" — is indecisive, for it is similar to many other references to their hope of the Lord's return.

POSTTRIBULATIONISM AND 2 THESSALONIANS 1:5-10

It is apparent from both Thessalonian epistles that the Christians in that city had undergone much persecution. This arose from the same causes that had forced Paul, Silas, and Timothy to flee Thessalonica for their lives. This suffering is mentioned in 1 Thessalonians 2:14; 3:3-5; and 2 Thessalonians 1:4,5. Paul exhorted the Christians to bear in mind that in due time God would punish their persecutors. He wrote,

> All this is evidence that God's judgment is right, and as a result you
> will be counted worthy of the kingdom of God, for which you are
> suffering. God is just: He will pay back trouble to those who trouble you
> and give relief to you who are troubled, and to us as well. This
> will happen when the Lord Jesus is revealed from heaven in

blazing fire with his powerful angels. He will punish those who do not know God and do not obey the gospel of our Lord Jesus. They will be punished with everlasting destruction and shut out in the presence of the Lord and from the majesty of His power on the day He comes to be glorified in his holy people and to be marveled at among all those who have believed. This includes you, because you believed our testimony to you   (2 Thess. 1:5-10 NIV).

Those who hold to a posttribulational rapture propose that the Thessalonians will be delivered at the end of the tribulation by the coming of the Lord, and that this is a contradiction of the pretribulational view. On the surface this seems plausible. However, in fact the Thessalonians were not delivered by the second coming of Christ and actually died before either the rapture or the tribulation time overtook the world. Posttribulationists explain this by saying that the Thessalonians are representative of the last generation of Christians — but how could this be a comfort to the Thessalonians in any realistic sense?

The pretribulational explanation is more cogent. The Thessalonians are being told that God in His own time will destroy their persecutors. Indeed, the persecutors of the Thessalonians will not be present at the second coming of Christ, for their resurrection is delayed until the end of the thousand years of the millennial kingdom. At that time they will be raised from the dead and cast into the lake of fire. Even if posttribulationists are correct, the judgment of the persecutors of the Thessalonians will not take place at the second coming of Christ. Only if the Thessalonians are taken as representative of the saints at the time of the second coming, and their persecutors are taken as representative of the wicked at the time of the second coming, can this passage have any relationship to a posttribulational rapture. Pretribulationists agree that when Christ comes in His second coming, He will punish unbelievers and deliver believers; yet they also hold that these believers will be, not members of the church, but those who have come to Christ subsequent to the rapture.

When all the factors are taken into consideration, the posttribulational argument falls apart because those who are actually punished at the second coming of Christ and the saints who are actually delivered are neither the persecutors of the Thessalonians nor are they necessarily members of the church, the body of

Christ. What is left is the comfort of certainty that God will deal with the wicked and in due time inflict divine judgment upon them. All in all, the passage does not contribute to the debate over the tribulation.

POSTTRIBULATIONAL INTERPRETATION
OF 2 THESSALONIANS 2:1-12

Both posttribulationists and pretribulationists claim that this chapter makes a major contribution to their point of view. Gundry writes a long chapter on his interpretation of 2 Thessalonians.[1] Ladd deals with it more briefly in his work.[2] Reese comments on it in scattered references throughout his volume.[3] In general these three teach that the great tribulation is placed specifically before the rapture of the church in this passage.

Chapter 2 of the epistle deals with the day of the Lord in relation to the man of sin. It opens with a reminder to the Thessalonians of their expectation of "the coming of our Lord Jesus Christ and our being gathered to him" (NIV). Apparently some false teachers had come to them teaching that they were already in the day of the Lord (v. 2). The King James Version refers to it as the day of Christ, but as practically all manuscripts read "Lord" instead of "Christ," there is general agreement that this is the proper reading. It is most significant that Paul here was writing because they had become alarmed at the thought that they were actually in the day of the Lord.

At the outset, posttribulationists have a real problem here. If the Thessalonians had been taught posttribulationism, the beginning of the day of the Lord would have been to them evidence that the rapture was drawing near and should have caused rejoicing. Instead of this, the beginning of the day of the Lord apparently created a panic in their midst, with the implication that before the false teachers had come they had understood that they would not enter this period. Paul continued,

> Don't let anyone deceive you in any way, for that day will not come until the rebellion occurs and the man of lawlessness is revealed, the man doomed to destruction. He opposes and exalts himself over everything that is called God or is worshiped, and even sets himself up in God's temple, proclaiming himself to be God. Don't

you remember that when I was with you I used to tell you these things? (vv. 3-5 NIV).

Paul asserts here that the Thessalonians were wrong in thinking that they were already in the day of the Lord, because there was a total lack of evidence for it. Two main evidences are mentioned: first, what the King James calls "a falling away" ("the rebellion" in NIV); second, that the man of lawlessness (NIV) or the man of sin (KJV) has not been revealed. Both of these would be necessary before the day of the Lord could really "come."

The word translated "the falling away" or "the rebellion" is from the Greek *apostasia*, from which the English word *apostasy* is derived. Some debate has arisen as to the exact meaning of this word, which could also be rendered "the departure." E. Schuyler English and others have suggested that the word means literally "departure" and refers to the rapture itself.[4]

Gundry argues at length against this interpretation, which would explicitly place the rapture before the day of the Lord, and his evidence is quite convincing. English is joined by the Greek scholar Kenneth S. Wuest, but their view has not met with general acceptance by either pretribulationists or posttribulationists.[5] A number of pretribulationists have interpreted the apostasy in this way as the departure of the church, but the evidence against this translation is impressive. In that case Gundry, seconded by Ladd, is probably right: the word refers to doctrinal defection of the special character that will be revealed in the day of the Lord. In this instance pretribulationists can agree with posttribulationists without agreeing with their conclusions on the passage as a whole.

The error into which the Thessalonians had fallen, according to Gundry, was one of two possibilities: "First, the Thessalonians, unaware of a pretribulational rapture, were led to believe that they had entered the tribulation, which they thought was part of the day of the Lord. . . . Second, the Thessalonians thought that a pretribulation rapture had already occurred and that they had been left behind in the tribulation, which (as in the preceding view) they believed to be a part of the day of the Lord."[6]

Gundry's second hypothesis — that the Thessalonians feared they had been left behind in the tribulation — makes sense only if the Thessalonians had been taught pretribulationism. If they were posttribulationists, there was no reason for concern; thus Gundry rejects that second hypothesis and its pretribulationist implications.

As a posttribulationist, Gundry holds that the pretribulational rapture view here is impossible because under the circumstances Paul, in correcting an error, would have made "a categorical statement to the effect that the rapture will take place before the tribulation. Such a statement nowhere appears."[7] Here, once again, Gundry argues from the silence of the passage.

The fact is that as the passage continues, Paul is not silent about the rapture intervening, if the passage is rightly interpreted. Nevertheless, Gundry goes on speculating for several more pages about the nature of the error of the Thessalonians. The crux of the matter, however, is found in Paul's discussion immediately following.

Beginning with verse 6, the apostle reminded them of what he had previously taught them: an event had to occur first before the man of sin could be revealed. Pretribulationists find in this a direct reference to the rapture as proof that the Thessalonians had the wrong point of view. Paul wrote,

> And now you know what is holding him back, so that he may be revealed at the proper time. For the secret power of lawlessness is already at work; but the one who now holds it back will continue to do so till he is taken out of the way. And then the lawless one will be revealed, whom the Lord Jesus will overthrow with the breath of his mouth and destroy by the splendor of his coming (2 Thess. 2:6-8 NIV).

Paul then describes further what will happen in connection with the coming of the lawless one.

Posttribulationists generally are quite divided as to the character of the one who is restraining or holding back evil. Gundry presents a chart indicating the various views that the restrainer is God, the Antichrist, or Satan, all views held by posttribulationists.[8] As Gundry goes on to state, a popular view is that the restrainer is the Roman Empire or government itself.

Unlike his fellows, Gundry agrees that the restrainer is the Holy Spirit, a view incompatible with posttribulationism. In support he offers evidence that this is an old view corroborated by the grammar and that the view is quite superior to the alternative views that the restraint is provided by the restrainer himself, be it the Roman Empire, human government today, or the Antichrist himself.

However, Gundry tries to part company with pretribulationists, who generally identify the restrainer as the Holy Spirit. He identifies the Holy Spirit as *in the church*, a point that pretribulationists have no problem accepting. Pretribulationists generally hold that if the Holy Spirit is removed from His present position indwelling the church, then the church itself must also be removed, and hence the rapture must take place at the same time.

If this removal of the Holy Spirit in the church takes place *before* the lawless can be revealed, it points to an event which must precede the tribulation. In a word, it is stating that the rapture precedes the tribulation.

In the discussion Gundry offers in support of his position, there is considerable confusion between the indwelling of the Spirit, the fullness of the Spirit, and the baptism of the Spirit. Gundry attempts to prove on the basis of Mark 13:11 that the Holy Spirit indwells His witnesses during the great tribulation; but the passage in Mark teaches the empowering of the Holy Spirit, saying nothing about indwelling. As a thorough student of dispensationalism, Gundry must certainly know that he is misrepresenting the pretribulational view. Pretribulationists hold that at the rapture we have a reversal of what occurs on the day of Pentecost — namely, that every believer was indwelt and baptized by the Spirit into the body of Christ. Certainly before Pentecost people were empowered by the Spirit and born again, even if they were not necessarily all indwelt or baptized by the Spirit.

Gundry's argument is unusually weak, and one almost senses in reading his discussion that he is aware of it. None of his proofs contradicting the concept that the Holy Spirit is removed with the church stand up under investigation. Pretribulationists agree that the removal of the Spirit is not complete, for the Holy Spirit is still omnipresent and still exercises some restraint, as the Book of Revelation makes plain in the protection of the 144,000. But neither Gundry nor anyone else can prove that the baptizing work of the Spirit which forms the church is ever seen in the tribulation. That the Spirit works in the tribulation all agree. That the Spirit indwells all believers in the tribulation is nowhere taught. Gundry, in making the concession that the Holy Spirit is the restrainer, has put himself in an untenable position to support posttribulationism in this passage. His statement "The usual pretribulational interpretation of 2 Thessalonians fails at every point" is simply not supported by the argument which he presents; neither is his broad statement, "At every point the posttribulational view of the passage commends itself."[9] This is pure dogmatism and is no substitute for solid argument. Actually it is impossible to harmonize Gundry's position on the Holy Spirit with posttribulationism.

Posttribulationism has failed to account for the alarm of the Thessalonians that they were already in the day of the Lord and the great tribulation. If they had been taught posttribulationism, they would not have been alarmed. The fact that Paul refutes it shows that they were in error in holding this position. If posttribulationism were right, Paul's approach to their correction could have been entirely different.

While posttribulationists and pretribulationists will continue to argue this passage, in reality there is nothing in it that teaches posttribulationism as such. Paul's correction of error begins in the very first verse of the passage by appealing to the Thessalonians' knowledge of the rapture; throughout the passage Paul appeals to their previous instruction in various points.

The exegesis of this passage reveals once again how Gundry has taken a position different from all preceding posttribulationists; if Gundry is right, then the preceding posttribulationists were wrong and vice versa. The common practice of counting up posttribulationists, and by their very numbers proving that posttribulationism is right, is based on the false premise that posttribulationists agree. As a matter of fact, they are quite diverse in their basic arguments and tend to contradict one another.

Notes

[1] Robert H. Gundry, *The Church and the Tribulation* (Grand Rapids: Zondervan Publishing House, 1973), pp. 112-28.

[2] George E. Ladd, *The Blessed Hope* (Grand Rapids: Wm. B. Eerdmans Publishing Co., 1956), pp. 73-75, 94-95.

[3] Alexander Reese, *The Approaching Advent of Christ* (London: Marshall, Morgan & Scott, 1937), pp. 126, 135, 166, 173, 244.

[4] E. Schuyler English, *Re-thinking the Rapture* (Travelers Rest, S. C.: Southern Bible Book House, 1954), p. 65.

[5] Kenneth S. Wuest, "The Rapture—Precisely When?" *Bibliotheca Sacra* 114 (January-March 1957): 69f.

[6] Gundry, *The Church and the Tribulation*, pp. 118-19.

[7] Ibid., p. 119.

[8] Ibid., p. 123.

[9] Ibid., p. 128.

Chapter 11

The Rapture in Relation to Endtime Events

Probably one of the most difficult problems a posttribulationist faces is to establish a well-defined order of events at the second advent. Posttribulationists tend to avoid this problem. Robert Gundry, more thaɩ others, makes an effort to state and solve the order of events. In the process, however, a number of acute problems in posttribulationism surface.

THE CONTRIBUTION OF 1 CORINTHIANS 15

Generally speaking, posttribulationists do not dwell at length on 1 Corinthians 15:51-58, one of the major passages on the rapture. The reason is obvious: this passage contributes nothing to the posttribulational argument and, in fact, poses a serious problem.

First Corinthians 15 is one of the great chapters of Scripture and in many respects it is the central chapter of this epistle. Because of the numerous problems, theological and moral, in the Corinthian church, Paul dwells on correction of these problems in the first fourteen chapters of 1 Corinthians.

When Paul comes to chapter 15, he develops the central aspect of his theology, the gospel with its testimony to the death of Christ for our sins and His resurrection. He then makes the practical application of the resurrection of Christ to our own faith and hope. The first fifty verses of 1 Corinthians 15 accordingly deal with the fundamental truths of the death and resurrection of Christ, and the resurrection of believers who die. Having laid this foundation, Paul then introduces the subject of the rapture of the church presented as "a mystery" in 1 Corinthians 15:51.

In referring to the rapture as a mystery, Paul is reaffirming that this is a New Testament truth not revealed in the Old Testament, a truth which, according to 1 Thessalonians 4:15, he had received by a special word from God. He summarizes what will happen at the rapture in 1 Corinthians 15:51,52: "Listen, I tell you a mystery: We shall not all sleep, but we shall all be changed — in a flash, in a twinkling of an eye, at the last trumpet. For the trumpet will sound, the dead will be raised imperishable, and we shall be changed" (NIV).

This revelation clearly confirms what had previously been revealed in 1 Thessalonians 4, but it adds some details. The rapture will occur in a moment of time. The dead who are raised will be given imperishable bodies. Living Christians will be changed and given bodies similar to those being raised from the dead. All this is in keeping with the principle laid down in 1 Corinthians 15:50 that our present bodies are not suited for heaven.

The rapture of the church is declared to be a great victory over death and a partial fulfillment of the Old Testament prophecies that the saints will have victory over death and the grave. On the basis of the fact of the return of Christ for His own, Paul exhorts the brethren in 1 Corinthians 15:58, "Therefore, my dear brothers, stand firm. Let nothing move you. Always give yourselves fully to the work of the Lord, because you know that your labor in the Lord is not in vain" (NIV).

In presenting the rapture in this passage, it should, first of all, be noted that Paul declared it to be a mystery. The doctrine of resurrection is no mystery, for it is clearly revealed in both the Old and New Testaments. The mystery was that living saints would be transformed at the time of the rapture and given a body suited for heaven without going through the experience of death. Although this had been anticipated in the Old Testament — in the case of Elijah and Enoch, who were translated and did not die —

there is no intimation in the Old Testament that such an event would take place when Christ returned to set up His kingdom. Accordingly the mystery is not resurrection, but translation of the living.

It should be clear to any reader of this chapter that Paul is presenting this truth as an imminent hope. On the basis of its expectation, he urges the brethren to serve the Lord faithfully. In that expectation, there is not a syllable of warning that their only hope of achieving this goal would be to pass through the coming time of great tribulation. Silence about a tribulation following the rapture is understandable if the rapture occurs first, but if the great tribulation precedes the rapture, it would have been cruel for the apostle to hold out the hope of the coming of the Lord for them when, as a matter of fact, it would be impossible unless they survived the tribulation.

First Corinthians 15 confirms what is uniformly true in all the rapture passages, that not a word of warning is ever given concerning a preceding tribulation. Posttribulationists tend to ignore this passage because to them it is a problem rather than a help in supporting their point of view. In the order of events, 1 Corinthians 15 confirms that the rapture comes first, before other great prophetic events will be fulfilled.

PRETRIBULATIONAL ORDER OF EVENTS

According to pretribulationists, the rapture of the church occurs at the end of the church age. It is followed by a period of adjustment in which a dictator and a ten-nation group emerge in the Middle East. Then a time of peace follows as this dictator enters into a treaty with Israel, indicated in Daniel 9:27 as intended to last for seven years. However, after the treaty has continued for three and one-half years, half its intended duration, the treaty is broken and the peacetime abruptly ends, followed by a period of persecution.

According to Daniel 9:27 and Matthew 24:15, the dictator in the Middle East desecrates the Jewish temple of that day, stops the sacrifices, and begins worldwide persecution of the Jew. Concurrently he rises to world power and becomes a world ruler (Rev. 13:7). He wields not only political power, but religious power (claiming to be God) and economic power (permitting no one to buy or sell without his permission — Rev. 13:8,17). Because he blasphemes God and persecutes the saints, the judgments of the great tribulation follow.

As the great tribulation progresses, major areas of the world begin rebelling against the dictator. A gigantic war erupts with great armies from the north, east, and south converging on the land of Palestine. At the height of this conflict, Jesus Christ returns in power and glory. He first destroys the armies who unite to fight the hosts of the Lord, as described in Revelation 19. The world ruler and the false prophet associated with him are cast into the lake of fire. Revelation 20 records that the martyrs of the tribulation will be raised from the dead, and many believe that the Old Testament saints will be resurrected at the same time according to Daniel 12:2. A series of judgments will follow that include both Jews and Gentiles and deal with their eligibility to enter the millennial kingdom.

Once these judgments are fulfilled, the millennial kingdom begins, and for a thousand years Christ reigns on earth. The millennium in turn is followed by the new heaven and the new earth and the eternal state. Because the rapture of the church in this point of view takes place before these endtime events, the pretribulationist has no need to find a place for it in connection with Christ's coming to earth. But posttribulationists have no such option and must find a suitable place for the rapture of the church among the events of the second coming.

THE POSTTRIBULATIONAL ORDER
OF EVENTS AT THE SECOND ADVENT

Posttribulationists seem to avoid itemizing events and their order at the second coming of Christ. Yet obviously, because the rapture is pictured as the church's meeting the Lord in the air, this must be inserted before Christ actually reaches the earth. As the heavenly hosts proceed from heaven to earth, the church, according to the posttribulationists, rises from earth and meets the Lord in the air; as the procession proceeds to the earth, the church joins with the coming King in extending His kingdom over the earth.

Amillenarians — who are uniformly posttribulationists because they deny a literal millennium — believe that Christ at His second coming introduces the new heaven and the new earth immediately after a general judgment of all men. They merge the judgment of the nations, the judgment of Israel, the judgment of the church, and the judgment of the great white throne as different aspects of the same event.

Premillenarians who are posttribulationists have certain problems. A most important fact all posttribulationists ignore is that the resurrection at the second coming is *after* the descent to the earth, not during the event, as Revelation 20:4 makes clear. This contradicts the posttribulational order of events.

If all the righteous are raptured and all the wicked are put to death, posttribulationists also face the problem of who will populate the millennial earth. In premillennialism there is general agreement that there will be people in the flesh on the earth who will live normal, earthly lives, bearing children, planting crops, building houses, living, and dying. Most premillenarian posttribulationists simply avoid this issue. Gundry is to be commended for making an effort to face this problem and attempt a solution. But his exegetical efforts to solve this problem also reveal the many complications a posttribulationist faces in ordering endtime events, so special attention should be directed to his contribution.

GUNDRY'S VIEW OF THE JUDGMENT OF THE NATIONS

Unlike most posttribulationists, who avoid it, Gundry confronts the problem of the judgment of the nations in Matthew 25:31-46. According to the text, this judgment will follow the second advent of Christ and the establishment of His throne. Many expositors recognize that the separation of the sheep and the goats is the separation of the saved from the unsaved on the basis of the evidence of their salvation and how they treat the Jew. Though at present unsaved people may be kind to Jews, in the great tribulation, with anti-Semitism at its height, anyone befriending the Jews described as "brothers" of the king would do so only because he is motivated by faith in Christ. Thus, while kind treatment of the Jew is not a ground for salvation, it is an evidence of it.

Gundry begins his objection to the normal pretribulational interpretation by citing the fact that in Matthew 12:50 — many chapters earlier than Matthew 25 — "Jesus defines His brothers as 'whoever shall do the will of My Father.' "[1] It seems to be extreme exegesis to take a reference thirteen chapters away, occurring in time two years before, as a specific definition. However, the major problem Gundry faces is determining where this judgment occurs in the sequence of events.

Virtually everyone except Gundry, whatever the eschatological viewpoint, considers the judgment of the nations as occurring approximately at the time of the second coming of Christ. This, however, poses a problem to posttribulationists because, if the rapture occurs while Christ is coming from heaven to the earth, it would automatically separate all believers from unbelievers. Then there would be no sheep (representing believers) intermingled with goats (representing unbelievers) on the earth when Christ sets up His throne.

Gundry attempts to resolve this difficulty by a number of divergent arguments. His ultimate solution is to place the judgment of the nations at the end of the millennium instead of the beginning. With it he also has to postpone the judgment seat of Christ until the end of the millennium. He argues that because the day of the Lord includes the millennium, there will be no problem in having the judgment at the end. He states, "Since the judgment of the wicked, admittedly postmillennial (Rev. 20:11-15), is joined with the second coming, nothing keeps the judgment of the righteous from being postmillennial, too."[2]

Gundry's statement that "nothing keeps the judgment of the righteous from being postmillennial" is, of course, not true. Gundry does not tackle the problems his view raises for premillennialism and posttribulationism. Matthew 25:35-39 pictures the "brethren" as naked, hungry, sick, and unjustly in prison. How could either Christians or Jews be in this predicament in the ideal state of the millennium, when there will be economic plenty and universal justice and when Israel will be especially blessed? The situation described is the great tribulation, not the millennial kingdom. It is another illustration of how Gundry ignores the main thrust of passages which he interprets.

While amillenarians tend to merge all the judgments just before the eternal state, premillenarians have seldom taken the position that the judgment of the nations is at the end of the millennium or that the judgment seat of Christ occurs at that time.

The reason for the majority of expositors other than Gundry taking this position that Matthew 25:31 expressly states that the action takes place "when the Son of man shall come in his glory." To interpret the action as occurring one thousand years later makes nonsense of this clause. It should be evident that Gundry is being forced to an extreme position in his effort to harmonize posttribulationism with the judgment of the nations. It is one of Gundry's weakest arguments.

GUNDRY'S INTERPRETATION OF THE BOOK OF REVELATION IN RELATION TO THE RAPTURE

Early in Gundry's treatment of the tribulation and the church, he devotes an entire chapter to his peculiar view of the Book of Revelation. He follows a relatively uncharted course as compared with other standard works on Revelation, yet in general he holds a futuristic viewpoint.

While it is unnecessary to take up all the details, attention can first be directed to his section on the rapture in Revelation 4:1,2. Though many pretribulationists find in the catching up of John a symbolic presentation of the rapture of the church, the passage obviously falls somewhat short of an actual statement of the rapture. Accordingly Gundry has some grounds for questioning the validity of this argument. In the process, he makes certain dogmatic statements that must be challenged. He states, for example, "The book of Revelation treats final events in fuller detail than does any other portion of the NT. Yet, not a single verse in Revelation straightforwardly describes a pretribulational rapture of the Church or advent of Christ."[3]

Pretribulationists rightfully are impatient with this kind of dogmatism because it is also true that the Book of Revelation nowhere describes a posttribulational rapture of the church. The last book of the Bible is specifically dealing with the second coming of Christ to the earth as its major theme, rather than with the rapture of the church as such; thus, if the rapture indeed is included in the second coming of Christ, the silence of Scripture on this point becomes more eloquent than the supposed silence of a pretribulational rapture. Gundry's repeated arguing from silence in his book is quite unwarranted unless he is willing to concede the validity of the argument from silence as it relates to pretribulationism. Yet he affirms the argument from silence over and over again when it suits his purpose for his viewpoint.

One of the familiar pretribulational arguments based on Revelation 3:10 is debated at length by Gundry.[4] Like most posttribulationists who discuss this subject, Gundry attempts to prove that the Greek preposition *ek* does not mean *from*, but *out from within*. The preposition, however, does not stand alone but is used with the verb *tereo*, normally translated *keep*. A parallel passage in usage is found in John 17:15, where Christ prays that His disciples may be protected from the evil one. Gundry points out that in our present experience we are not taken out of the world but protected from the evil of the world.

What Gundry and most posttribulationists do not take into consideration is that the Bible expressly reveals that saints in the great tribulation will not be protected, except in certain rare instances such as the 144,000, and that the only way they can be kept "from the hour of trial" (NIV) of the great tribulation is by being removed.

Accordingly, while Gundry displays a great deal of erudition in his discussion, it is another illustration of evading the most important point. The promise to the Philadelphian church was not that they would be kept *through* the tribulation. The promise, "I will also keep you *from the hour of trial* that is going to come upon the whole world to test those who live on the earth" (NIV, italics added). The point is that they were promised to be kept from the time period of the tribulation.

Gundry discusses the word *hour* referring to the prayer of Christ in John 12:27 — "Father, save me from this hour?" (NIV) — arguing that it is not simply a time period. Here again Gundry misses the point. The fact is, the Father did not save Christ from the hour, that is, the time of suffering. While Gundry states the posttribulational argument as well as it can be stated, it still falls short of proof that this is what Revelation 3:10 really means.

The problem of this passage turns somewhat on the question of whether the Philadelphian church is typical of the true church, the body of Christ. This may be debated, but the fact remains that even the Philadelphian church as it was historically in existence in the first century could not have been promised that they would be kept "from the hour of trial that is going to come upon the whole world to test those who live on the earth" (Rev. 3:10, NIV) if, as a matter of fact, posttribulationism is the correct view. All agree that the Philadelphian church died before the tribulation began, but the question is whether the promise was valid. Pretribulationists can claim this text for whatever application is relevant. While the extent of its support of pretribulationism may be debated, it does not offer any proof at all for the posttribulational view. The issue is whether the church is kept *through* the tribulation or kept *from* this period. The Greek preposition *dia* should have been used if the concept of *through* were intended.

Gundry, like many others, debates whether the twenty-four elders stand for the church. This is an issue that most scholars agree cannot be finally determined. If the Textus Receptus is correct, then the twenty-four elders are clearly the church, as the first person is used in the song of the redeemed in Revelation 5:9,10. If, however, this is changed to the third person as other texts read, it leaves the question open as to whether these are angels or men. Thus, while the passage offers no support for the posttribulational view, the support for the pretribulational view remains under question.

There is, however, the inference that the elders are wearing crowns of reward, and this implies that their judgment has already taken place. If they are angels, this is inexplicable, for it is quite clear that the judgment of angels is later. If they are the church and the church has been raptured earlier, then the rewards make sense. Gundry's argument — that if the crowns imply rapture, then John's being caught up could not symbolize the rapture — may point out an inconsistency, but for those pretribulationists who do not regard John's being caught up as the rapture, it is no clear refutation. Whatever evidence there is about the twenty-four elders is in favor of pretribulationism, not against it. This probably explains why Gundry devotes five pages to this rather tenuous argument. All that posttribulationists can do at this point is to raise questions; they cannot prove that the pretribulationists are wrong in their identification of the elders as the church.

To harmonize the Book of Revelation with posttribulationism, Gundry has his own way of combining the seals, trumpets, and bowls of the wrath of God. According to his diagram, the trumpets begin with the fourth seal; the bowls begin with the fourth trumpet; the seventh seal, the seventh trumpet, and the seventh bowl are simultaneous. All this is quite arbitrary, but it is hardly necessary to debate all the issues involved in order to determine whether the Book of Revelation is in harmony with the pre- or posttribulational position. Gundry's position gives him a good deal of flexibility and tends to help him in his idea that the day of the Lord does not begin until the end. It should be evident to any reader, however, that Gundry is arranging the Book of Revelation to harmonize with posttribulationism and his peculiar view of it rather than interpreting it on exegetical considerations.

The usual pretribulational argument that the church is not mentioned in Revelation 4–18 calls for four pages of Gundry's discussion.[5] Some of Gundry's arguments may have partial relevance and force. But the fact remains that the church is not mentioned in this period. This does not prove pretribulationism, but it certainly poses a problem for posttribulationism which Gundry does not solve.

Probably the most important divergent view of Gundry is his interpretation of the 144,000 in Revelation 7:1-8 and 14:1-5. Practically all posttribulationists spiritualize these twelve tribes that constitute the 144,000 as representing spiritual Israel, viz., the church. Because he distinguishes Israel from the church Gundry cannot use this method of equating the 144,000 with the church.

Gundry may be right that the 144,000 are not necessarily preachers of the gospel, but he tends to ignore the evidence that they are genuinely saved. He refers to them as bondservants (Rev. 7:3), significantly omitting a reference to the fact that they are servants "of God." Thus Gundry offers the suggestion that the 144,000 are a Jewish remnant who are unsaved, who are not members of the church, and who are not raptured. He holds that when the rapture occurs and they see their Messiah descending to the earth, they suddenly are converted.

The Scriptures Gundry cites (Zech. 3:8,9; 12:9–13:1; Mal. 3:1-5; Rom. 11:26,27) simply do not support the concept that there is a second chance for people on earth who are unsaved at the time of Christ's return. Most posttribulationists disagree with Gundry here. While Gundry attempts to establish this point of view, it is a weak argument. As far as the writer knows, no one in the history of the church has ever held that the 144,000 are unsaved, orthodox Jews. They hold either that they are members of the church and are converted or, as pretribulationists usually hold, that they are saved Israelites. Gundry further holds that the 144,000 "will include both men and women who will populate and replenish the millennial kingdom of Israel."[6]

While both posttribulationists and pretribulationists agree that there will be a godly remnant of Israel awaiting Christ at His return, Gundry's view of the 144,000 is absolutely unique and is another evidence of his somewhat desperate attempts to harmonize his very unusual views of posttribulationism with the Book of Revelation.

Gundry also spends some time refuting the view that the marriage supper of the lamb in Revelation 19 is another evidence for a pretribulation rapture. In a normal Oriental wedding, three stages can be observed — first, the legal stage; second, the bridegroom's coming for the bride; and third, the wedding feast. Pretribulationists stress that, if in Revelation 19 the wedding feast is announced, the two preceding stages, including the bridegroom's coming for the bride, has already been accomplished. Gundry replies, "To press woodenly the marital relationship of both Israel and the Church to the Lord would be to say that God is a bigamist."[7] Such a statement suggests that Gundry is straining too hard to try to explain a point which, after all, is not decisive. Whatever weight this may have, it is no help to the posttribulationist.

GUNDRY'S VIEW OF ARMAGEDDON

A peculiarity of Gundry's view is that he does not believe the

·day of the Lord begins until Armageddon. Although Armageddon is clearly the last hour preceding the second coming of Christ, Gundry would have us believe that none of the judgments preceding Armageddon are judgments of the day of the Lord. Gundry states, "Certain celestial portents will both precede the day of the Lord (Joel 2:30,31) and follow immediately upon the tribulation (Matt. 24:29). Clearly, the day of the Lord will not begin with the tribulation or any part of it, for otherwise the heavenly portents after the tribulation could not be said to precede that day."[8]

The logic of these and succeeding statements, as well as Gundry's rather tangled argument in support of his contention, are all open to question. The facts are that the Book of Revelation, beginning in chapter 6, makes very clear that there are a series of "celestial portents" and that they occur throughout the whole period, as well as in the climax that marks its close. Most readers will find Gundry's argument hard to understand at this point.

The Book of Revelation teaches that God will pour out His judgments on the earth over a period of years preceding Armageddon and that all of these judgments are properly a description of what the Bible describes as the day of the Lord. Even if we shuffle the various events of the Book of Revelation to suit Gundry's view, as he attempts to do, it still comes through clearly that judgments of the day of the Lord occur long before Armageddon; with this comes the evidence that the day of the Lord itself is under way. Since this is one of Gundry's principal contentions and the view on which his whole superstructure rests, the questionable character of his evidence weakens his entire agrument. If the Book of Revelation teaches anything, it teaches that God's judgments fall upon the earth beginning at chapter 6 and culminating in chapter 19. For most readers Gundry's view will not make sense.

POSTTRIBULATIONISM AT ITS WEAKEST POINT

As the discussion of the rapture in relation to the endtime events has indicated, the problem of ordering events is a major one for posttribulationism and especially for the view of Robert Gundry. All posttribulationists stumble when trying to place the rapture in the order of events at the endtime because it does not fit naturally into the sequence. Amillenarians have less trouble than premillenarians. But posttribulationists are trying to establish an event not indicated in any passage dealing with the second coming of Christ to the earth and without causal relationship to the events which follow.

The problem is compounded by Gundry's attempt to combine dispensationalism with posttribulationism. His view as a whole stands or falls on three major issues: (1) his view of the judgment of the nations; (2) his view of the 144,000; and (3) his view of Armageddon as preceding the beginning of the day of the Lord. It is not too much to say that Gundry's position is unique and is rather clearly the product of his problems in coordinating the endtime events. If Gundry is wrong in placing the judgment of the nations at the end of the millennium — as practically all expositors would hold — and if he is wrong in identifying the 144,000 as unsaved orthodox Jews who nevertheless are "servants of God," and if he is wrong in his attempt to delete all the judgments of God which precede Armageddon as not being in the day of the Lord, then his conclusions are also wrong. The ordinary posttribulational teachings that the judgment of the nations takes place at the second coming of Christ, that the 144,000 represent saved individuals, and that divine judgments fall on the earth before Armageddon are far more tenable than Gundry's point of view.

Nevertheless the problem of all posttribulationists comes out more graphically in Gundry than in any other posttribulational interpreter. The rapture of the church just does not fit endtime events unless it is made the first in the series and before the tribulation. The unique views of Gundry actually pose more problems to the posttribulationist than they do to the pretribulationist.

In attempting to relate the rapture to endtime events, the deep-seated problems of posttribulationism surface again and again. The basic problem of posttribulationists — that their theological inductions are not based on all the facts and that they tend to be selective in their supporting evidence, ignoring the problems — leaves their conclusions in question. Because of the comprehensive nature of scriptural revelation in both the Old and New Testaments on endtime events, for there to be a complete omission of the rapture in connection with the second coming of Christ becomes a most difficult problem. Gundry's argument is complicated by his attempt to be literal, which only results in entangling him in various conclusions which are unique to him and a practice of using principles that do not lead to his conclusions. If posttribulationism stands or falls on the reasonableness of his analysis of endtime events, it ought to be clear that posttribulationism fails to support its major contentions.

Notes

[1] Robert H. Gundry, *The Church and the Tribulation* (Grand Rapids: Zondervan Publishing House, 1973), p. 166.

[2] Ibid., p. 170

[3] Ibid., p. 69.

[4] Ibid., pp. 54-61.

[5] Ibid., pp. 77-81.

[6] Ibid., p. 82.

[7] Ibid., p. 85.

[8] Ibid., p. 95.

Chapter 12

Unresolved Problems of Posttribulationism

In the study of the relative merits of arguments supporting pretribulationism and posttribulationism, it becomes evident that not all the arguments for either conclusion are necessarily decisive. If either the pretribulational or posttribulational rapture was unequivocably taught in Scripture, it is doubtful whether worthy scholars would divide on the question. The conclusions reached necessarily are based on the total weight of the supporting evidence and the extent to which each view solves its problems.

Pretribulationists continue to believe that, on the whole, they have offered a better solution to the exegesis of the New Testament on the subject of Christ's coming for His church than the posttribulationists. Posttribulationists continue to hold that pretribulationists have not firmly established their point of view.

SUMMARY OF POSTTRIBULATIONAL ARGUMENTS

Most posttribulational arguments are in the nature of refutation of pretribulationism. Posttribulationists, however, have approached the subject from at least four major points of view, as mentioned previously, and both the premises and the supporting evidence vary a great deal. A summary of the more important arguments is helpful in weighing the relative merits of posttribulationism and pretribulationism. Because of variations in posttribulational interpretation, however, these need to be divided into two classes: (1) arguments on which posttribulationists agree; (2) arguments on which posttribulationists themselves disagree.

POSTTRIBULATIONAL ARGUMENTS ADVANCED BY ALL POSTTRIBULATIONISTS

1. *Historical argument.* Practically all posttribulationists charge that pretribulationism is a recent theory which surfaced in the writings of J. N. Darby about 150 years ago. Accordingly they argue that posttribulationism is the standard doctrine of the church, and they raise the question why pretribulationism was not advanced earlier if it is actually the teaching of Scripture. George E. Ladd, for instance, devotes a third of his book to the historical argument, and practically every writer on posttribulationism emphasizes and reemphasizes this point.[1] In offering this argument, posttribulationists generally ignore the fact that most modern forms of posttribulationism differ greatly from that of the early church or of the Protestant Reformers and are actually just as new or perhaps newer than pretribulationism.

2. *The argument from silence.* Practically all posttribulationists appeal to the fact that the New Testament does not state in so many words a pretribulational rapture. Here they frequently refer to the Olivet Discourse (Matt. 24–25), which does not mention the rapture in its list of endtime events. They also argue that in the rapture passages there is no clear statement of the great tribulation following the event. Writers like Robert Gundry repeat over and over this argument from silence as one of the most convincing arguments for posttribulationism.[2] Almost invariably omitted, however, is the confession that the Bible is also silent on a posttribulational rapture and never mentions the great tribulation as preceding the rapture. It is a curious note that posttribulationists consistently deny pretribulationists the right to use the argument from silence while using the same argument to support their own viewpoints.

As pointed out in the previous discussion, the silence about a rapture in major passages minutely describing the endtime is much more damaging to posttribulationism than the apparent similar silence in regard to a pretribulational rapture. The point is that if the rapture is imminent, it does not demand any further explanation, but if the rapture follows the great tribulation, it necessarily would require a warning to those facing this time that this would be what they could expect.

3. *Argument from the Olivet Discourse.* Most posttribulationists appeal to Matthew 24–25 as proof of a posttribulation rapture. In addition to noting that the rapture is not placed before the great tribulation, they find in Matthew 24:40,41 an explicit reference to the rapture as occurring at the end of the great tribulation. They tend to ignore the pretribulational explanation of this passage, which denies that there is a rapture at this point.[3] In Matthew 25, practically all posttribulationists ignore their problem of explaining the judgment of the nations — with the notable exception of Gundry, who attempts to solve the problem by placing the judgment at the end of the millennium.[4]

4. *Argument from terminology relating to the return of the Lord.* Because of the similar terminology for the rapture and the second coming of Christ to the earth, posttribulationists usually argue that the two events must be one and the same unless they are clearly revealed to be distinct in the Scriptures. Here they attempt to make technical such words as *coming, appearing,* and *revelation,* which are general not technical terms. Without exception they ignore the fact that the Old Testament presented the first and second comings of Christ in a similarly confusing terminology which was impossible to differentiate until the New Testament was written.

5. *Argument from the wheat and the tares.* Posttribulationists generally call attention to the fact that in Matthew 13:30 the tares are taken up first before the wheat. Here they beg the question because the passage is not talking about the rapture; actually they create a problem for themselves, because it contradicts their own sequence of events of a posttribulational rapture. In posttribulationalism the wicked are not dealt with finally before the rapture either. With the exception of Gundry, they uniformly ignore the changed order of the separation of the good and bad fish in Matthew 13:48-50. There is a constant tendency among posttribulationists to be selective in the facts chosen from eschatological passages.

6. *The argument from the day of the Lord.* Most posttribulationists note the close proximity of the day of the Lord to the doctrine of the rapture in 1 Thessalonians 4–5. They argue that if the day of the Lord introduces the second coming of Christ after the tribulation, then the rapture must also be after the tribulation. Here their argument has weight only if they can prove that the day of the Lord begins at the conclusion of the great tribulation. While there are problems for both pretribulationists and posttribulationists in this passage, the evidence supports the conclusion that the day of the Lord begins much earlier than the close of the great tribulation, and if so, then the rapture also must be much earlier.

7. *Argument from the doctrine of the restrainer in 2 Thessalonians 2.* Posttribulationists with this passage usually appeal to the argument from silence, that if the pretribulational rapture were an established truth, Paul would have settled the doctrinal difficulty the Thessalonians faced by reasserting pretribulationism. Posttribulationists are rather slow to admit that pretribulationists have actually established this point in the interpretation of the restrainer as the Holy Spirit. This would set up a chronology of the removal of the Holy Spirit and the church first, to be followed by the revelation of the man of sin and the tribulation. Apart from the argument of silence, posttribulationists do not have much to work on in this passage.

8. *Argument from the posttribulational resurrection.* Most posttribulationists call attention to the expression "first resurrection" in Revelation 20:4-6. They argue, how could a posttribulational resurrection be "first" if a rapture had actually taken place before the tribulation? Here posttribulationists almost without exception overlook the problems that this presents to their own view, as all agree that Christ was raised from the dead first. There is a notable lack of recognition of the problems of this view and of the actual meaning of the word *first* to designate the resurrection which is *before* the resurrection of the great white throne, not in the sense of the first resurrection to take place in history.

As pointed out earlier, the resurrection of Revelation 20:4-6 actually occurs *after* the second coming of Christ and therefore contradicts the idea that the rapture in the posttribulational view is a part of the second coming of Christ from heaven to earth. Even a posttribulationist would have to recognize that in his order of events, the resurrection of Revelation 20:4-6 is not "first."

9. *Posttribulational argument from terminology.* In addition to claiming that various words used interchangeably for the rapture and the second coming are technical words, posttribulationists like Alexander Reese argue that terms such as "the end" can refer to only one event and therefore make impossible a pretribulational rapture.[5] In advancing this argument, posttribulationists are notably lacking in proof that the terms claimed to be technical are actually so used in Scripture. Pretribulationists counter this argument by insisting that the context must be taken into consideration, and that the context does not support the posttribulationists' technical definition of the terms.

POSTTRIBULATION ARGUMENTS IN WHICH POSTTRIBULATIONISTS THEMSELVES DISAGREE SUBSTANTIALLY

Because posttribulationism exists in at least four different schools of thought, it is natural that their arguments against pretribulationism should differ in keeping with their points of view. It is important to note that these differences are not minor, but major, in which to some extent posttribulationists refute each other.

1. *Disagreement on the nature of the tribulation.* Posttribulationists like J. Barton Payne, following the lead of some of the early church fathers and the Protestant Reformers, completely spiritualize the great tribulation, making it a contemporary or past event.[6] Thus, under this view, posttribulationists affirm the imminency of Christ's return in keeping with the viewpoint of the various rapture passages. Payne's viewpoint is probably the predominant view of church history until the last two centuries; recent posttribulationists like Ladd and Gundry argue for a future tribulation. While the principles of interpretation adopted by Ladd and Gundry are far superior to that of Payne, because they deal with prophecy as subject to literal fulfillment, as posttribulationists they also must face a series of problems which a literal, future great tribulation introduces.

2. *Disagreement on the doctrine of imminency.* Posttribulationists are disagreed as to the nature of the imminency of the Lord's return. Payne holds that Christ could return at any moment and therefore that the rapture and the second coming are imminent. Most contemporary posttribulationists, however, see specific prophecies as still unfulfilled, including the emergence of the Antichrist, the great tribulation, and Armageddon. They are confronted with the problem that the rapture passages seem to indicate an imminent rapture in contrast with these specific events which must precede Christ's second coming to the earth. In an attempt to dissolve this difference, posttribulationists try to redefine imminence as merely indicating a return of Christ *soon* and argue against the idea that the rapture could occur at any moment. Here posttribulationists tend to ignore the note of imminency in Scripture and in the history of the church in relation to the return of Christ.

3. *Disagreement on the nature of the suffering of the saints in the great tribulation.* Posttribulationists who accept a literal great tribulation are confronted with the problem of harmonizing this with promises of comfort in 1 Thessalonians 4 and a blessed expectation of the Lord's return in Titus 2:13. While Payne solves this problem by spiritualizing the great tribulation, those who take it literally must find some other explanation. Generally they tend to minimize the sufferings and to insulate the saints from the judgments of the great tribulation. Here posttribulationists flounder badly, and their major disagreement on the nature of the tribulation creates serious problems.

4. *Disagreement on the Book of Revelation.* A major problem of posttribulationists is that they have no uniform interpretation of the Book of Revelation. Many posttribulationists spiritualize the great judgments described in Revelation 6–19, while others attempt to take them somewhat literally. Most posttribulationists spiritualize the 144,000 of Israel as representing saints in general and tend to make Israel and the church the same spiritual entity. Gundry offers a unique interpretation, differing from other posttribulationists in portraying the 144,000 as orthodox Jews who are unsaved until the moment of the rapture.[7] Because of the wide variety of viewpoints among the posttribulationists on the Book of

Revelation, their arguments are conflicting and contradictory.

5. *Disagreement on the nature of the church.* Most posttribulationists tend to spiritualize the church as including saints of all ages. They argue that saints are in the great tribulation and therefore the church must go through it. Gundry is the exception to this in that he attempts to distinguish between the church and Israel in most instances. Most posttribulationists recognize that a major ground for pretribulationism is the distinction between the church and Israel; posttribulationists like Gundry, however, take an opposite view. The result is further confusion in the posttribulational argument.

6. *Disagreement on a second chance for unbelievers at the second coming of Christ.* Gundry and a few others attempt to resolve the problem of saints in the millennium still in their natural bodies — in contrast with the saints raptured after the tribulation — by teaching a second chance to be saved after the rapture. While pretribulationists can point to an extended number of years during which people could come to Christ and qualify to enter the millennium in their natural bodies, posttribulationists do not generally postulate a second chance for those who are unbelievers at the time of the rapture. Gundry is one of the few who advance this position, which is unsupported in Scripture.

7. *Disagreement as to a specific order of events at the time of the second coming.* Posttribulationists rarely offer a specific sequence of events in connection with the second coming of Christ. Although obligated to include the rapture in the descent of Christ from heaven to the earth, most of them do not defend it or explain it. The reason for this is that the rapture is, for them, an extraneous note in the events described in the second coming of Christ to the earth, and it introduces problems in the various Scriptures dealing with divine judgments. For instance, the resurrection of the tribulation saints is placed after Christ returns to earth, not in the process of His descent.

8. *Disagreement on the nature of the judgments at the second coming of Christ.* While posttribulationists agree that there are judgments at the second coming of Christ, they disagree as to their time and order. Gundry places the judgment of the nations and the judgment seat of Christ at the end of the millennium.[8] Post-

tribulationists usually lump the various judgments at the second coming and if premillennial, place them before the millennium. There is no uniform teaching among posttribulationists on the final judgments.

9. *Disagreement on the millennium.* Posttribulationists are not agreed as to whether premillennialism, postmillennialism, or amillennialism is the correct view. Accordingly posttribulationism does not lend itself to a single system of eschatological interpretation and varies widely in its concept of the fulfillment of prophecy. It is difficult to find two posttribulationists who agree completely on the order of endtime events.

RESULTING UNRESOLVED POSTTRIBULATIONAL PROBLEMS

In most studies of posttribulational arguments, it is often overlooked that posttribulationists have not really solved their major problems. These fall into three major areas: (1) the silence of Scripture on crucial facts of posttribulationism; (2) the obvious contrasts between passages dealing with the rapture and passages relating to the second coming of Christ to the earth; (3) problems of contradiction, or teachings of posttribulationism that conflict with normal premillennial interpretation of Scripture. While these problem areas in posttribulationism have been considered in various chapters in this book, the force of them becomes more evident when they are summarized.

SILENCE OF SCRIPTURE ON FACTS CRUCIAL
TO POSTTRIBULATIONISM

Posttribulationists usually make much of the charge that pretribulationism is based only on inference. Although the charge is partly true, they cover up the fact that posttribulationism is also based on inference.

First, posttribulationists have never been able to prove that the church as the body of Christ is actually in the period of tribulation, especially the one designated in Scripture as the "great tribulation." All agree that in the great tribulation there are people, referred to as "saints," who are saved Israelites or saved Gentiles. None of the usual terms is used such as the word *church* or synonyms which include both Jew and Gentile as the distinctive body of saints in the present age. Posttribulationists attempt to solve this by making Israel and the church the same or by using other evasive arguments. But they cannot cite a single passage that incontrovertibly places the church the body of Christ in the great tribulation. While the argument from silence has its limitations, it is strange that in the extended description of the great tribulation as found in Revelation 4-18, there is not a single reference to the church as being in the period. While posttribulationists have worked hard to place the church in the Olivet Discourse and have otherwise attempted to counter the force of this argument, the fact remains that they have never satisfactorily explained this.

Second, posttribulationists have never satisfactorily explained why the Thessalonian Christians were not warned of the coming great tribulation when the hope of the rapture was extended to them as a comfort.

Writers like James Montgomery Boice, for instance, find the argument of 1 Thessalonians 4 sufficiently convincing to settle the question of pretribulationism and posttribulationism. Boice says,

> According to this [posttribulational] view, the church of Jesus Christ *will* go through the great tribulation, after which Jesus will return for those believers who are remaining. In reply, it is enough to note that, although the church has gone through periods of great persecution in the past and undoubtedly may go through greater and even more intense persecutions before Christ's return, nevertheless, the view of a posttribulational rapture is impossible for the simple reason that it makes meaningless the very argument that Paul was presenting in the Thessalonian letters. Paul was arguing for the imminence of Christ's return. This is to be the major source of comfort for suffering believers. If Christ will not come until after the great tribulation (that is, a special period of unusual and intense suffering still in the future), then the return of the Lord is not imminent and tribulation rather than deliverance is what we must anticipate.[9]

The attempts of posttribulationists to make this the comfort of resurrection ring hollow if, in fact, the Thessalonians had to go through the great tribulation before they could experience either resurrection or translation. Posttribulationists have not solved their problem in 1 Thessalonians 4.

Third, posttribulationists have not resolved the problem that the apostle Paul, in teaching the doctrine of the rapture to the Corinthians, obviously exhorted them on the basis of the imminency of the Lord's return without any warning whatever of an impending great tribulation (1 Cor. 15:51-58). While the posttribulational problem of 1 Corinthians 15 is not so acute as the problem of 1 Thessalonians 4, it is equally pertinent to ask why the doctrine of the great tribulation is not taught when the context would seem to require it. Every passage that clearly relates to the rapture has this unusual feature of exhortation which is based on the imminency of the rapture and the absence of any warning of an intervening great tribulation.

Fourth, posttribulationists have never established the crucial fact that a translation of living saints and the specific resurrection of the church occur at the time when Jesus Christ comes back to establish His kingdom. Here again various evasive tactics are followed, such as trying to equate the church with the martyred saints of Revelation 20:4. The argument is all in favor of the pretribulational view because, if the resurrection included all the church, if would not be necessary to specify the resurrection of the martyred dead of the last generation who were killed by the beast.

In like manner in the graphic and complete description of the second coming of Jesus Christ in Revelation 19, there is no indication whatever that the procession will be met by the raptured church rising from earth to meet the Lord in the air. There is no indication of either resurrection or translation occurring in the process of Christ's descent to the earth. The implication clearly is that the tribulation saints will be raised *after* Christ has come and started to establish His kingdom on earth, not while He is descending from heaven to the earth. Posttribulationists are left with no text whatever to support placing the rapture in this sequence of events.

If the Scriptures are silent on placing the church the body of Christ in the tribulation, and if the rapture truth is presented in such a way that it requires imminency to make sense out of the exhortation, and if the scriptural accounts in all passages where Christ is clearly coming from heaven to earth in His second coming omit any reference either to the resurrection of the church

or to the translation of the living — all this leaves posttribulationists open to the charge that they have not proved these
central doctrines crucial to their position.

THE PROBLEM OF CONTRASTING DETAILS OF THE RAPTURE AND THE SECOND COMING OF CHRIST

Posttribulationists tend to ignore or evade the obvious fact
that the rapture is presented as an event entirely different from the
second coming of Christ to set up His kingdom. Although they can
properly point to the fact that much the same terminology is used,
since both refer to a "coming" and a "revelation" of Jesus Christ,
the details supplied in passages relating to the rapture and the
second coming contrast sharply.

First, in all the passages on the rapture, no preceding signs
are given, for the rapture is always presented as an imminent
event. By contrast, major passages on the second coming of Christ
such as Matthew 24:27-31 and Revelation 19:11-21 clearly picture
the great tribulation preceding, and on this virtually all interpreters agree. Signs preceding the second coming of Christ include a
definite sequence of important, world-shaking events described in
the Old Testament and the New Testament, including the
emergence of a ten-nation confederation in the Middle East, the
rise of a world ruler, and a climactic world war under way at the
time of the second advent. None of these items is ever mentioned
in connection with the rapture of the church. In addition, Scriptures make clear that there will be great disturbances in the
heavens and great catastrophes on earth, including earthquakes,
famine, pestilence, and great loss of life, all of which constitute the
horrors of the great tribulation. The second coming clearly is
preceded by these events, but not a single passage dealing with the
rapture ever anticipates such.

Second, details of the rapture vary considerably from the
details of the second coming. At the rapture, saints meet Christ in
the air, while at the second coming of Christ, the meeting with
saints on earth follows His arrival on the Mount of Olives.

Third, as far as any rapture passage is concerned, there are
no fundamental changes in the world situation at the rapture,
while at the second coming there are devastating changes includ-

ing the cleavage of the Mount of Olives (Zech. 14:4,5).

Fourth, all agree that living saints are translated, and the dead in Christ are raised at the rapture. In no passage is there mention of translation at the second coming, and the saints who are raised are not identified with the church.

Fifth, posttribulationists have not satisfactorily explained John 14 with its promise of taking the saints to the Father's house. At the rapture, saints will fulfill this promise; at the second coming to the earth, there is no translation and no departure to the Father's house.

Sixth, when the rapture occurs, there is no indication of worldwide judgment, though it is followed by the judgment seat of Christ for the church. By contrast, at the second coming the whole world is judged, including both Jew and Gentile, saved and unsaved living on the earth.

Seventh, at the rapture there is no indication that a millennial reign of Christ immediately follows. But major passages on the second coming of Christ picture the world, not only as judged, but as established in righteousness in Christ's kingdom on the earth.

Eighth, indications from 1 Thessalonians 5 point to the conclusion that the church will be delivered *before* the time of wrath overtakes the world, while at the second coming the deliverance comes for those who have believed in Christ during the tribulation *after* they have gone through this time of wrath.

Ninth, in keeping with the peculiar character of the church as the body of saints in the present age, the truth relating to the rapture is found only in the New Testament. This contrasts with events related to the second coming that are the subject of much prophecy in both the Old and New Testaments.

Tenth, at the rapture there is no judgment upon the nation Israel, as far as any rapture passage is concerned. But at the second coming of Christ it is clear that Israel is judged, with the rebels purged, and the saved in Israel ushered into the millennial kingdom (Ezek. 20:34-38).

Eleventh, at the rapture there is no judgment of the nations, while all agree that the judgment of the nations occurs after the second coming of Christ.

Twelfth, at the rapture there is no mention of any judgment on Satan, or of Satan's being bound as a consequence of the coming of Christ for His church. But it is clear that at the second coming of Christ, Satan is bound and rendered inoperative for the thousand-year reign (Rev. 20).

Thirteenth, the rapture is always presented as an event imminent to this church age. The fact that certain predictions which Christ made have been fulfilled in the present age is not a serious problem, for there is no intervening event necessarily taking place before the rapture of the church today. By contrast, the second coming of Christ to establish His kingdom must be preceded by major events covering an extended period of time.

Fourteenth, no two events could be more dissimilar than the rapture of the church and the second coming of Christ to set up His kingdom. There is as much difference between the rapture and Christ's future coming to the earth as there is between the first coming and the second coming of Christ. They involve the same person, Jesus Christ, but the details attributed to the two events in Scripture are entirely different.

Although the problems of contrast are not all equally important, their total weight is such that it leaves posttribulationism without an adequate explanation. Posttribulationism has not given a satisfactory answer to these crucial contrasts.

THE POSTTRIBULATION PROBLEM
OF CONTRADICTORY INTERPRETATIONS

As discussed earlier, posttribulationists are not agreed among themselves as to how to resolve some of their contradictions. While they have made an earnest effort to resolve their problems — often by redefining the terms to their own point of view and being selective in what they choose to note in central passages — it remains that posttribulationism has inherent contradictions, especially if the premillennial viewpoint be adopted.

First, these problems surface in such passages as 1 Thessalonians 5, where posttribulationists have to give a particular interpretation to the day of the Lord which is not supported by its usage in the Old and New Testaments. While pretribulationists have not been without fault in their interpretation of this phrase, the posttribulationists have certainly not solved the problem.

Second, posttribulationists have never come up with a satisfactory explanation of how the restrainer must be removed before the man of sin can be revealed. Although the exegesis of 2 Thessalonians 2 is not without its difficulties, as was pointed out in the discussion of this passage, the interpretation that the restrainer is the Holy Spirit in relationship to the church is superior to any other. If this is the case, then posttribulationists have a real problem of harmonizing this with their view.

Third, as illustrated by Gundry's treatment of the time of wrath, posttribulationists are hard put to explain how the church can go through a day of wrath and yet have comfort with the thought of translation at its end. Posttribulationists disagree among themselves as to how to solve this problem. Some of them spiritualize the great tribulation, as does J. Barton Payne[10]; others try to evade the problem by declaring that while the world is the object of divine wrath, the church is not. Gundry's position — that the great tribulation is a time of satanic wrath — complicates rather than helps his position, as satanic wrath is vented only on believers, not on unbelievers. Posttribulationists have not solved this problem and have not offered convincing answers.

Fourth, posttribulationists who are premillennial have not solved the problem of transition from the tribulation to the millennium. According to Scripture, survivors of the tribulation — both Jews and Gentiles who are saved — enter the millennium in their natural bodies. They are described as having normal functions as people living in the flesh on earth. If so, posttribulationists have a major problem in explaining how these could be raptured and still have natural bodies. Most posttribulationists choose to ignore this, as do Ladd and Reese.[11]

Gundry, as we have seen, attempts to solve the problem by a complicated explanation unique in the history of interpretation, but he actually never resolves the difficulty. It is not too much to say that this is one of the major problems of posttribulationism if premillennialism is assumed. How can saints go into the millennium in their natural bodies if, in fact, they were raptured while Christ was coming from heaven to the earth? Gundry's postulate of a second chance at the second coming is without any scriptural support.

CONCLUSION

It is too much to say that the stated objections to the post-tribulational view prove that the pretribulational interpretation is right. But they certainly give adequate ground for the pretribulationist to reject posttribulationism. The pretribulational view offers a better explanation of key problems and passages than does posttribulationism. The fact that posttribulationists avoid their major problems is in itself a confession that in crucial areas they have not supported their conclusions. For this reason, along with the positive testimony of the truth of the rapture in the New Testament, pretribulationists continue to hold that the coming of Christ for His saints is imminent, an event that precedes the tribulation period as a blessed, comforting, and purifying hope.

Just as the distinctions between the first and second comings of Christ were not fully apparent to all until the first coming took place, so it is probable that the church at large will not recognize the distinction between the rapture and the second coming until the rapture itself takes place. Meanwhile, those who depend on Scripture relating to these unfulfilled prophetic events will need to weigh the evidence for these contradictory views. Both cannot be true, and the question can only be resolved by searching the Scriptures dealing with this prophetic hope.

Notes

[1] George E. Ladd, *The Blessed Hope* (Grand Rapids: Wm. B. Eerdmans Publishing Co., 1956).

[2] Robert H. Gundry, *The Church and the Tribulation* (Grand Rapids: Zondervan Publishing House, 1973).

[3] See chapter 7, "Do the Gospels Reveal a Posttribulational Rapture?"

[4] Gundry, *The Church and the Tribulation,* pp. 166-71.

[5] Alexander Reese, *The Approaching Advent of Christ* (London: Marshall, Morgan and Scott, 1937), pp. 120-24.

[6] J. Barton Payne, *The Imminent Appearing of Christ* (Grand Rapids: Wm. B. Eerdmans Publishing Co., 1962).

[7] Gundry, *The Church and the Tribulation,* pp. 81-83.

[8] Ibid., pp. 163-71.

[9] James Montgomery Boice, *The Last and Future World* (Grand Rapids: Zondervan Publishing House, 1974), pp. 41-42.

[10] Payne, *The Imminent Appearing of Christ.*

[11] Ladd, *The Blessed Hope;* Reese, *The Approaching Advent of Christ.*

Chapter 13

Pretribulationism as the Alternative to Posttribulationism

Throughout the preceding discussion of posttribulationism, the superiority of the pretribulational view to posttribulationism has been pointed out. Although it is not the purpose of this volume to present pretribulationism as such, as this has been done in the author's *The Rapture Question*,[1] a summary of pretribulationism is in order.

CLARITY OF PRETRIBULATIONAL PREMISES

As demonstrated in the preceding discussion, posttribulationism is faulty in its statement of its premises. Because posttribulationists are largely in confusion in their basic presuppositions, they are open to the charge of contradiction and illogical reasoning. By contrast, pretribulationists bring into focus the major issues that relate to eschatology.

1. *The authority and accuracy of Scripture.* While conservative posttribulationists usually concur with pretribulationists on the authority and accuracy of Scripture, they lack the unanimity evident in all pretribulationists in their doctrine of the Scriptures. It is not uncommon for scholars who defect from pretribulationism in favor of posttribulationism to also defect in their doctrine of the inerrancy of Scripture.

2. *Principle of literal interpretation of prophecy.* Among post-

159

tribulationists there is a wide divergence on the issue of the basic principles of biblical interpretation, especially as related to prophecy. Even conservative interpreters like J. Barton Payne, as previous discussion has demonstrated, spiritualize prophecies when they seem to contradict posttribulationism. Robert Gundry, who attempts a literal interpretation of prophecy, spiritualizes when a literal interpretation would contradict posttribulationism. Lack of consistency among posttribulationists in principles of interpretation have undoubtedly contributed to their lack of agreement among themselves and confusion on important points in posttribulationism. Pretribulationists do not need to spiritualize prophecy in order to support the pretribulational rapture and are more consistent in their application of the principle of literal interpretation of prophecy.

3. *The church contrasted with Israel.* Although Robert Gundry is a major exception, most posttribulationists fail to distinguish the scriptural program for the church, the body of Christ, and the program of God for Israel. The confusion of Israel and the church is one of the major reasons for confusion in prophecy as a whole, as illustrated in both amillennialism and posttribulationism. Robert Gundry attempts to distinguish Israel and the church, but in order to support his posttribulationism he has to invent some novel explanations, as previous discussion has pointed out. Only in pretribulationism is the distinct program for the church clearly defined.

4. *A literal future tribulation.* Posttribulationists are quite at odds among themselves as to the nature of the tribulation, some holding that it is a literal future period, and others that it is already past. Pretribulationism holds with clarity to a future great tribulation and to a literal fulfillment of the events and situations which will characterize this period. One of the principal causes for confusion among the posttribulationists is their lack of consistency on the subject of the future tribulation.

Arguments for Pretribulationism

As presented in the author's *The Rapture Question*, there are at least fifty arguments for pretribulationism.[2] Many of these have been alluded to in the preceding discussion. For the purpose of establishing a suitable summary, some of the more important arguments can be restated.

1. *Contrasts between the rapture and the second coming.* Probably the most important reason for pretribulationism is the evident contrast between the details revealed concerning the rapture and the description given of the second coming of Christ to establish His kingdom. As itemized in the preceding chapter, these contrasts describe these two events as different in purpose, character, and result.

As previously noted, an analogy can be drawn between the contrasts in the Old Testament between the first and second comings of Christ, and the contrasts in the New Testament between the rapture and the second coming of Christ to the earth. In the Old Testament, the first coming and second coming of Christ were mingled, but can now be distinguished because of the major contrasts of the sufferings of Christ relating to His first coming and the glory of Christ relating to His second coming.

It is doubtful whether anyone comprehended the difference between the first and second comings of Christ until the prophecies of the first coming were fulfilled. In interpreting the distinctions between the rapture and the second coming of Christ, interpreters do not have the benefit of fulfilled prophecy as a basis of interpretation, but the same approach which enables us to distinguish the first coming from the second coming of Christ enables us to distinguish the rapture from the second coming to the earth.

Only the pretribulational interpretation can account for these sharp contrasts and the literal interpretation of the various factors relating to these two future events. Inevitably posttribulationists are forced to spiritualize to some extent in order to explain away the evident contrast.

2. *Silence of Scripture on a posttribulational rapture.* Posttribulationists tend to make much of the fact that the Scriptures, in presenting the rapture, do not provide an ordered sequence of events which states in so many words that the rapture is first and the tribulation follows. Many eschatological problems, of course, would be resolved if the Scriptures specifically stated, for instance, that Christ's coming is premillennial or if in the Old Testament it

clearly outlined the first coming of Christ to be followed by the present church age and then the second coming of Christ. The form of divine revelation given to us in Scripture does not always provide such an itemization.

While the argument from silence is never conclusive, most posttribulationists are not willing to admit that the silence in Scripture concerning a posttribulational rapture is much more significant than the silence in Scripture concerning the tribulation following the rapture. While no passage attempts to relate the rapture to a sequence of events, the second coming of Christ is revealed in a detailed way.

In Matthew 24, as well as in Revelation 4–19, specific revelation of events leading up to the second coming and a description of the second coming of Christ itself is provided. In view of this itemization, it is therefore most significant that the rapture is never mentioned at all when many other events are itemized. Accordingly, the rhetorical question of posttribulationists as to where the Bible teaches a pretribulation rapture actually boomerangs on the posttribulationist because he is unable to come up with any statement of a posttribulational rapture, even though the events preceding and following the second coming are given in great detail.

In the argument from silence, posttribulationists also attempt to evade the fact that the church, the body of Christ, is never mentioned in a tribulation passage. Many posttribulationists spiritualize the tribulation and make the church equivalent to the saints of all ages. The complete silence of the Scriptures on the subject of the church as such in the great tribulation has considerable weight. On the whole, the argument from silence is more damaging to the posttribulational view than it is to the pretribulational interpretation.

3. *Imminence of the rapture.* As presented in all major passages on the rapture, the coming of Christ for His church is uniformly presented as an imminent event. This is in sharp contrast to the presentation of the doctrine of the second coming, which is consistently presented as following a sequence of events — including the return of Israel to the land, the rise of the dictator in the Middle East (sometimes referred to as the Antichrist), and the forty-two

months of the great tribulation detailed in the Book of Revelation. The second coming of Christ to the earth in no proper sense can be called an imminent event, even though posttribulationists strain to redefine the English word as meaning something other than an event which is immediately pending. Only by complete spiritualization of the major events leading up to the second coming of Christ can this problem be avoided by posttribulationism, and in this spiritualization a major principle of proper interpretation of eschatology is sacrificed.

The claim of many contemporary posttribulationists that they represent the historic position of the church is true only if they spiritualize the tribulation. Futurists like Ladd and Gundry offer a position that is quite different from the early church fathers' and, as a matter of fact, it is more recent than pretribulationism as is commonly taught today. The fact that the rapture is presented as an imminent event is a major argument for distinguishing the rapture from the second coming of Christ to the earth.

4. *The doctrine of a literal tribulation.* Pretribulationists regard the great tribulation as a future event and rightly place the rapture as occurring before this time of unprecedented trouble. By contrast, there is complete confusion among the posttribulationists on this point and an amazing lack of uniformity in applying the principles of interpretation. Posttribulationists are caught in the twin problem of either carrying the church through the great tribulation with resulting martyrdom for probably the majority of the church, or spiritualizing the period and thereby introducing the principles of interpretation that lead not only to posttribulationism, but to amillennialism and a denial of any reasonable order of events for the endtime.

The difficulty of harmonizing the rapture as the blessed hope with the prospect of martyrdom and the problem of maintaining premillennialism while holding to posttribulationism has continued to plague some of the major interpreters of the posttribulational view. By contrast, the pretribulation view offers a clear and simple explanation. The blessed hope is the rapture of the church before the great tribulation. The second coming of Christ to the earth follows the tribulation. Pretribulationists accordingly are not forced to spiritualize or to evade the plain teaching of

Scripture on the subject of the rapture or of the great tribulation.

5. *An ordered chronology of events.* The pretribulational interpretation allows the interpreter of both the Old and New Testaments to establish an order for endtime events that makes sense. While many details may not be revealed, the major events of the endtime as commonly held by pretribulationists can be established. By contrast, it would be difficult to find two posttribulationists who agree on any system of events relating to the endtime. The reason for confusion among the posttribulationists is a lack of uniformity in principles of interpretation that results in disagreements as to the extent of spiritualization required. While large prophecy conferences are held by pretribulationists with evident agreement of the speakers on major events of the endtime, no such conference has ever been held by posttribulationists for the simple reason that they do not have any major agreement among themselves. Accordingly prophecy conferences are almost the exclusive domain of the pretribulational interpretation.

Because of the confusion among posttribulationists as to how endtime events should be ordered, it is natural that there should be confusion on the interpretation of prophecy as a whole — and this is exactly what the contemporary theological scene reveals. While pretribulationism is a single system of interpretation on major events, posttribulationism is divided among many schools of interpretation, with great variation, even on major events. Pretribulationism continues to be the key to establishing a system of eschatological interpretation.

6. *Exhortations relating to the rapture harmonized with pretribulationism.* An important basis for pretribulationism is found in the nature of the exhortations given in connection with the revelation of the rapture. In John 14, the disciples were exhorted, "Let not your heart be troubled" (v. 1). If it were evident that they would have to go through the great tribulation first, they had every reason to be troubled. As a matter of fact, most of the disciples had already died as martyrs when the apostle John recorded the words of John 14. It was evident that he is repeating these great promises because of their application to the church as a whole in keeping with the general revelation of the upper room discourse in John 13–17.

In a similar way, the exhortation of 1 Thessalonians 4:18 extending comfort to the Thessalonians in the deaths of their loved ones, in harmony with the possibility of the return of Christ for them at any time, would be devoid of any real meaning if they had to go through the great tribulation first. While many generations of Christians have died before the rapture, it is evident that the exhortation given to the Thessalonians applies to each succeeding generation which continues to have the bright hope of an imminent return of the Lord for His own.

The exhortations of the major passage on the rapture in 1 Corinthians 15:51-58 are similar in their implications. Not a word of warning is given concerning a coming tribulation, but they are exhorted to be living in the light of the imminent return of Christ. This hope is defined by Paul in Titus 2:13 as "that blessed hope, and the glorious appearing of the great God and our Saviour, Jesus Christ." The hope of a rapture after enduring the great tribulation is hardly a happy expectation, and this passage is difficult for posttribulationists to explain. The hope is not that of resurrection after death and martyrdom, but rather the coming and revelation of Christ in His glory to them while they are still living on the earth. The exhortations relating to the rapture constitute a major problem to posttribulationism.

7. *The rapture in relation to premillennialism.* Posttribulationists who are premillennial are caught in the vise of a dilemma. If they spiritualize the great tribulation to avoid the problems of harmonization with a posttribulational rapture as J. Barton Payne does, they are adopting principles of interpretation that lead logically to amillennialism, which spiritualizes not only the tribulation but the millennium itself. If, as premillenarians, they take the great tribulation literally, then they have the problem of harmonizing the imminence of the rapture and exhortations relating to it with a posttribulational rapture. The dilemma facing posttribulationism accounts for the general confusion that exists among them on endtime events.

Logically, posttribulationism leads to amillennialism and pretribulationism leads to premillennialism. Any compromise between these two points of view leads to confusion in principles of interpretation as well as in the interpretation itself. The obvious difficulty in moving from a posttribulational rapture into a millennium with saints on earth who have not been raptured forces interpreters like Gundry to postulate a second chance for salvation after the rapture, a doctrine nowhere taught in Scripture and expressly denied in the Book of Revelation (Rev. 14:9-11).

The evident trend among scholars who have forsaken pretribulationism for posttribulationism is that in many cases they also abandon premillennialism. For those who wish to think consistently and logically from principles to interpretation, the options continue to be (1) a pretribulational rapture followed by a premillennial return of Christ to the earth, or (2) abandoning both for a posttribulational rapture and a spiritualized millennium. It becomes evident that pretribulationism is more than a dispute between those who place the rapture before and after the tribulation. It is actually the key to an eschatological system. It plays a determinative role in establishing principles of interpretation which, if carried through consistently, lead to the pretribulational and premillennial interpretation.

ADVANTAGES OF PRETRIBULATIONISM

By way of summary, three major considerations point to the advantages of the pretribulational point of view.

1. *Pretribulationism, a logical system.* While writers in all schools of biblical interpretation can be found who are guilty of illogical reasoning, careful observers of posttribulationism will find that so often their conclusions are based upon illogical reasoning. In some cases, their arguments hang upon dogmatic assumptions which they do not prove. In other cases, they draw conclusions from Scripture passages under consideration which the passages actually do not teach. The fact that an interpreter is a great scholar does not necessarily make him a logician; unfortunately, ability to do research and skill in linguistics do not necessarily lead to formation of logical conclusions. The writer believes that a major problem in posttribulationism is logical inconsistency. By contrast, pretribulationism moves logically from its premises and principles of interpretation to its conclusion.

2. *Exegetical advantages of pretribulationism.* In contrast with posttribulational treatment of major passages on the rapture which differs widely in interpretation, pretribulationists follow a

consistent pattern of literal or normal interpretation. This allows the interpreter to explain the passage in its normal meaning — which in many cases is its literal meaning — without resorting to flagrant spiritualization in order to avoid pointed contrast between the rapture and the second coming of Christ to the earth.

It is rather significant that, without any attempt to establish uniformity in eschatology, the Bible Institute movement of America is predominantly premillennial and pretribulational. This has come from taking Scripture in its plain, ordinary meaning and explaining it in this sense. By contrast, educational institutions that have approached the Bible creedally tend to make Scriptures conform to their previously accepted creed with the result that most of them are liberals or, if conservative, tend to be amillennial.

Pretribulationism has continued to appeal to thousands of lay interpreters because it makes sense out of the passages that deal with the rapture of the church. While the majority of biblical scholars may disagree with pretribulational interpretation, it is also significant that they disagree radically among themselves as well; often abandonment of pretribulational interpretation results in abandonment of serious study in the area of prophecy.

3. *Practical advantages.* In all the major rapture passages, the truth of the coming of the Lord is connected with practical exhortation. While it is undoubtedly true that eternal values remain in other interpretations, only the pretribulationists can consistently hold to a moment-by-moment expectation of the Lord's return along with the literal interpretation of the promises that are to be fulfilled following the Lord's coming. For the pretribulationist, the coming of the Lord is an imminent hope. For the great majority of others, there is only the somewhat blurred expectation of how the coming of the Lord really fits in to the pattern of future events. It is for this reason that pretribulationists hold tenaciously to their point of view, defend it earnestly, and believe the doctrine of the imminent return of Christ an important aspect of their future hope.

Notes

[1] Walvoord, John F., *The Rapture Question* (Findlay, Ohio: Dunham Publishing Co., 1957).

[2] Ibid., pp. 191-99.

Bibliography

Albright, W. F., and Mann, C. S. *The Anchor Bible*, vol. 26, *Matthew*. Garden City, N. Y.: Doubleday Co., 1971.

Alford, Henry. *The Greek Testament*, 4 vols. Chicago: Moody Press, 1958.

Allen, Willoughby C. "A Critical and Exegetical Commentary on the Gospel According to Saint Matthew." In *International Critical Commentary*, 3rd ed. Edinburgh: T&T Clark Co., 1907.

Allis, Oswald T. *Prophecy in the Church*. Philadelphia: Presbyterian and Reformed Publishing Co., 1945.

Anderson, Sir Robert. *The Coming Prince*. Grand Rapids: Kregel Publications, 1954.

Armerding, Carl. "The Coming of the Son of Man," *Moody Monthly*, 51 (1951): 787-88, 809.

———. *The Olivet Discourse*. Findlay, Ohio: Dunham Publishing Co., 1955.

Arndt, William F., and Gingrich, F. Wilbur. *A Greek-English Lexicon of the New Testament*. Chicago: University of Chicago Press, 1957.

Boice, James Montgomery. *The Last and Future World*. Grand Rapids: Zondervan Publishing House, 1974.

Buis, Harry. *The Book of Revelation*. Philadelphia: Presbyterian and Reformed Publishing Co., 1960.

Chafer, Lewis Sperry. *Systematic Theology*. 8 vols. Dallas: Dallas Seminary Press, 1948.

———. *Major Bible Themes*. Revised by John F. Walvoord. Grand Rapids: Zondervan Publishing House, 1974.

Darby, J. N. *Notes on the Apocalypse*. London: G. Morrish, 1842.

Douty, Norman F. *Has Christ's Return Two Stages?* New York: Pageant Press, Inc., 1956.

Ellicott, Charles J. *A Critical and Grammatical Commentary on St. Paul's Epistle to the Thessalonians*. Andover: Warren F. Draper, 1864.

English, E. Schuyler. *Re-Thinking The Rapture*. Travelers Rest, S. C.: Southern Bible Book House, 1954.

Erdman, Charles R. *The Epistles of Paul to the Thessalonians*. Philadelphia: Westminster Press, 1935.

Frame, James Everett. "A Critical and Exegetical Commentary on the Epistles of St. Paul to the Thessalonians." In *The International Critical Commentary*. New York: Scribner, 1912.

Fromow, George H. *Will the Church Pass Through the Tribulation?* London: Sovereign Grace Advent Testimony, n.d.

Frost, Henry W. *Matthew Twenty-four and the Revelation*. New York: Oxford University Press, 1924.

Gaebelein, Arno C. *The Gospel of Matthew*, 2 vols. New York: Our Hope Publishing Office, 1910.

————. *The Harmony of the Prophetic Word*. New York: Our Hope Publishing Office, 1907.

————. *The Revelation*. New York: Our Hope Publishing Office, 1915.

Grant, F. W. *The Revelation of Jesus Christ*. New York: Loizeaux Brothers, n.d.

Guthrie, Donald. *New Testament Introduction*. Downers Grove, Ill.: Inter-Varsity Press, 1971.

Harnack, Adolph von. *History of Dogma*, trans. Neil Buchanan. 7 vols. New York: Dover Publications, 1961.

Harrison, William K. "The Time of the Rapture as Indicated in Certain Scriptures," *Bibliotheca Sacra*, 114 (1957): 316-25; 115 (1958): 20-26, 109-19, 201-11.

Hendriksen, William. "Exposition of I and II Thessalonians." *New Testament Commentary*. Grand Rapids: Baker Book House, 1955.

————. *More Than Conquerors*. Grand Rapids: Baker Book House, 1939.

Hiebert, D. Edmond. *The Thessalonian Epistles*. Chicago: Moody Press, 1971.

Hodge, Charles. *Systematic Theology*. 3 vols. New York: Charles Scribner's Sons, 1895.

Hogg, C. F., and Vine, W. E. *The Epistles of Paul the Apostle to the Thessalonians*. Reprint. Grand Rapids: Kregel Book House, 1959.

Huebner, R. A. *The Truth of the Pre-Tribulation Rapture Recovered*. Millington, N. J.: Present Truth Publishers, 1973.

Ironside, Henry Allen. *Expository Notes from the Gospel of Matthew*. New York: Loizeaux Brothers, 1948.

————. *Lectures on the Book of Revelation*. New York: Loizeaux Brothers, 1930.

Kelly, William. *Lectures in the Gospel of Matthew*, 5th American ed. New York: Loizeaux Brothers, 1943.

————. *Lectures on the Book of Revelation*. London: W. H. Broom, 1874.

————. *The Epistles of Paul the Apostle to the Thessalonians*. 3rd ed. London: C. A. Hammond, 1953.

Knudten, Richard D. *The Systematic Thought of Washington Gladden*. New York: Humanities Press, 1968.

Kuyper, Abraham. *The Revelation of St. John*, trans. John Hendrik de Vries. Grand Rapids: Wm. B. Eerdmans Publishing Co., 1935.

Ladd, George E. *Jesus and the Kingdom*. New York: Harper and Row, Publishers, 1964.

————. *The Blessed Hope*. Grand Rapids: Wm. B. Eerdmans Publishing Co., 1956.

Larkin, Clarence. *Book of Revelation*. Philadelphia: Published by the author, 1919.

Lenski, R. C. H. *The Interpretation of St. John's Revelation*. Columbus, Ohio: Lutheran Book Concern, 1935.

————. *The Interpretation of St. Matthew's Gospel*. Minneapolis: Wartburg Press, 1943.

————. *The Interpretation of St. Paul's Epistles to the Colossians, to the Thessalonians, to Timothy, to Titus, and to Philemon*. Columbus, Ohio: Lutheran Book Concern, 1937.

Lightfoot, J. B., *Notes on the Epistles of Saint Paul from unpublished commentaries*. London: Macmillan and Co., 1895.

Lindsey, Hal, et al. *When Is Jesus Coming Again?* Carol Stream, Ill.: Creation House, 1974.

Lloyd-Jones, D. Martyn. *Studies in the Sermon on the Mount*, 2 vols. Grand Rapids: Wm. B. Eerdmans Publishing Co., 1959.

MacPherson, Dave. *The Incredible Cover-Up*. Plainfield, N. J.: Logos International, 1975.

MacPherson, Norman F. *Triumph Through Tribulation*. Otego, N. Y.: First Baptist Church, 1944.

Morgan, G. Campbell. *The Gospel According to Matthew*. New York: Fleming H. Revell Co., 1929.

Morris, Leon. *The Epistles of Paul to the Thessalonians*. Grand Rapids: Wm. B. Eerdmans Publishing Co., 1957.

Ockenga, Harold J. *The Church in God*. Westwood, N. J.: Fleming H. Revell Co., 1956.

Payne, J. Barton. *The Imminent Appearing of Christ*. Grand Rapids: Wm. B. Eerdmans Publishing Co., 1962.

Pentecost, J. Dwight. *Things to Come*. Findlay, Ohio: Dunham Publishing Co., 1958.

Plummer, Alfred. *An Exegetical Commentary on the Gospel According to St. Matthew*. London: Robert Scott Roxburgh, 1909.

————. *A Commentary on St. Paul's First Epistle to the Thessalonians*. London: Robert Scott, 1918.

————. *A Commentary on St. Paul's Second Epistle to the Thessalonians*. London: Robert Scott, 1918.

Ramm, Bernard. *Protestant Biblical Interpretation*. Boston: W. A. Wilde Co., 1958.

Rand, James F. "A Survey of the Eschatology of the Olivet Discourse," Parts I-II, *Bibliotheca Sacra*, 113 (1956): 162-73, 200-13.

Rauschenbusch, Walter. *A Theology For The Social Gospel*. New York: Macmillan Co., 1922.

Reese, Alexander. *The Approaching Advent of Christ*. London: Marshall, Morgan, Scott, 1932.

Ritschl, Albrecht. *The Christian Doctrine of Justification and Reconciliation*. Ed. H. R. MacKintosh and A. B. MacAulay. Clifton, N. J.: Reference Book Publishers, 1966.

Rose, George L. *Tribulation till Translation*. Glendale, Calif.: Rose Publishing Co., 1942.

Ryrie, Charles C. *First and Second Thessalonians*. Chicago: Moody Press, 1959.

Sandeen, Ernest R. *The Roots of Fundamentalism*. Chicago: University of Chicago Press, 1970.

Sauer, Erich. *From Eternity to Eternity*. Grand Rapids: Wm. B. Eerdmans Publishing Co., 1954.

Scofield, C. I. *The Scofield Reference Bible*. New York: Oxford University Press, 1917.

Scroggie, W. G. *The Book of Revelation*. Edinburgh: The Book Stall, 1920.
————. *A Guide to the Gospels*. London: Pickering and Inglis, 1948.

Seiss, Joseph A. *The Apocalypse*. Grand Rapids: Zondervan Publishing House, 1957.

Scott, Walter. *Exposition of the Revelation of Jesus Christ*. London: Pickering and Inglis, n.d.

Smith, J. B. *A Revelation of Jesus Christ*. Scottdale, Pa.: Herald Press, 1961.

Stanton, Gerald B. *Kept From the Hour*. Grand Rapids: Zondervan Publishing House, 1956.

Strombeck, J. F. *First the Rapture*. Moline, Ill.: Strombeck Agency, Inc., 1950.

Strong, Augustus Hopkins. *Systematic Theology*. 7th ed. Philadelphia: A. C. Armstrong and Son, 1902.

Summers, Ray. *Worthy Is The Lamb*. Nashville: Broadman Press, 1951.

Swete, Henry B. *The Apocalypse of St. John*. Grand Rapids: Wm. B. Eerdmans Publishing Co., n.d.

Tappert, Theodore G., ed. *Luther's Works*, 56 vols. Philadelphia: Fortress Press, 1967.

Tasker, R. Z. G. *The Gospel According to Matthew*, Tyndale Bible Commentary. Grand Rapids: Wm. B. Eerdmans Publishing Co., 1961.

Tenney, Merrill C. *The Book of Revelation*. Grand Rapids: Baker Book House, 1963.

Thiessen, Henry Clarence. *Will the Church Pass Through the Tribulation?* New York: Loizeaux Brothers, 1941.
————. "Will the Church Pass Through the Tribulation?" *Bibliotheca Sacra*, 92 (1935):39-54, 187-205, 292-314.

Thomas, W. H. Griffith. *Outline Studies in the Gospel of Matthew*. Grand Rapids: Wm. B. Eerdmans Publishing Co., 1961.

Walvoord, John F. "A Review of *The Blessed Hope* by George E. Ladd." *Bibliotheca Sacra* 113 (Oct., 1956): 289-307.

————. *Matthew: Thy Kingdom Come*. Chicago: Moody Press, 1974.

————. "Premillennialism and the Tribulation." *Bibliotheca Sacra* 112 (Apr., 1955): 97-106.

————. *The Millennial Kingdom*. Grand Rapids: Zondervan Publishing House, 1959.

————. *The Thessalonian Epistles*. Findlay, Ohio: Dunham Publishing Co., 1955.

————. *The Rapture Question*. Findlay, Ohio: Dunham Publishing Co., 1957.

————. *Revelation of Jesus Christ*. Chicago: Moody Press, 1966.

Warfield, B. B. *Biblical Doctrines*. New York: Oxford University Press, 1929.

West, Nathaniel, ed. *Premillennial Essays*. New York: Fleming H. Revell Co., 1879.

Wood, Leon J. *Is the Rapture Next?* Grand Rapids: Zondervan Publishing House, 1956.

Wuest, Kenneth S. "The Rapture — Precisely When?" *Bibliotheca Sacra*, 114 (1957): 68-69.

Subject Index

Allis, Oswald *18, 19*

Amillennialism *7;* major views of *13, 14;* rise of *12, 13*

Antichrist, problem of posttribulational interpretation *26, 27*

Argument for dispensational posttribulationism *61-63*

Argument for posttribulationism, summary of, as advanced by all posttribulationists *145-48*

Argument from inference, in posttribulationism *51-53*

Argument from silence, in posttribulationism *145, 146, 151-54*

Arguments on which posttribulationists disagree *148-51*

Armageddon *140, 141*

Assumption that rapture is posttribulational *63, 64*

Boice, James Montgomery *152*

Calvin, John *74*

Church as the elect *34, 35;* contrasted to Israel *160;* deliverance of church from tribulation according to posttribulationism *55;* Gundry on *53, 67;* Ladd on *52, 53;* mysteries of, according to Gundry *65, 66;* nature of *150;* Rose on *53;* twenty-four elders *138*

Classic posttribulationism *21-29;* summary of classic posttribulationism *28, 29*

Darby, J. N. *44, 47, 48, 145*

Day of Christ *119, 120*

Day of the Lord *108-20, 147;* in the Old Testament *111-13;* in 1 Thessalonians 5 *115-20;* in 2 Thessalonians 2 *124, 125*

Death in relation to rapture *94, 95*

Dispensationalism as related to posttribulationism *55, 56, 60-68;* dispensational posttribulational exegesis of Gospels *82-93;* posttribulational opposition to dispensationalism *64-68*

Elders, twenty-four *138, 139*

Endtime events *148, 150*

English, E. Schuyler *125*

Eschatology, development of *12, 13*

Evidence, lack of in posttribulationism *39*

Exhortation to watch *54*

Fromow, George H. *35*

Futurist posttribulationism *40-59;* as a recent view *40;* premises of *40, 41;* problems of *58, 59*

Gundry, Robert H. *19, 31, 44, 53, 60-68, 70-80, 82-93, 96-100, 113-20, 124-28, 134-43, 145, 146, 157, 166*

Hiebert, D. Edmond *106, 116*

Historical argument for posttribulationism *145;* a half-truth *42;* claim to be historic view *32, 33;* claim to be orthodox view *18;* Gundry's new view of *68;* in early church *17;* in Protestant Reformation *17;* in recent posttribulationism *32, 33, 68;* rejection by posttribulationism of view of early church *24, 25, 32, 33, 68*

Huebner, R. A. *44, 46*

Improper use of induction in amillennialism and postmillennialism *9, 15, 16*

Interpretation, principles of in posttribulationism *8, 9, 159;* dual hermeneutics of Augustine *12*

Interpretation of John 14 *91, 92*

Interpretation of 1 Thessalonians 4 *96-106*

Interpretation of 2 Thessalonians 2 *122-28;* problems of interpretation in Gundry *62*

Irving, Edward *42-45*

Israel as the church in posttribulationism *34*

Judgments, at second coming *150, 151;* of angels *138;* of the nations *84;* of the nations in Gundry's view *134-36;* of the wicked *84, 85*

Key passages on posttribulationism *80*

Ladd, George *18, 19, 22, 31, 40-59, 65, 98, 104, 105, 124, 145, 148, 157*

Luther, Martin *74;* on the tribulation *36, 37*

MacDonald, Margaret *42-46*

MacPherson, David *42-48*

MacPherson, Norman S., on the tribulation *34*

Marriage supper of the lamb *140*

Midtribulationism *7*

Millennium *151;* problem of populating in posttribulationism *53*

New Covenant, Gundry's view *66*

Olivet Discourse *85-90, 146*

One hundred forty-four thousand *139, 140*

Order of prophetic events, problem in posttribulationism *38, 58, 133, 134*

Payne, J. Barton *17, 21-24, 31, 44, 71, 72, 74, 91, 104, 105, 148, 149*
Pentecost, J. Dwight *64*
Postmillennialism, rise of *14*
Premillennialism *7;* historical development of *12, 13;* major doctrines of *15;* rise to prominence *15*
Pretribulationism, advantages of *166, 167;* arguments for *160-66;* as a blessed hope *9, 10;* as a logical system *166;* as opposed to postribulationism *7;* as recent *42-48;* as the most satisfactory view *9, 159-67;* clarity of premises *159, 160;* exegetical advantages of *166, 167;* hope of escaping the tribulation *75;* in the Olivet Discourse *86, 87;* in 1 Corinthians 15 *130-32;* in 1 Thessalonians 4 *96-101;* in 1 Thessalonians 5 *117, 118;* in 2 Thessalonians 2 *123, 127;* in Book of Revelation *136-40;* practical advantages of *167;* providing ordered chronology of events *132, 133, 164*
Problem of defining the nature of the rapture *99, 100;* of harmonizing differing views *16;* of ordering predicted events preceding the second coming *26, 141-43;* of relating premillennialism to posttribulationism *28*
Problems of posttribulational interpretation of Daniel 9 *26;* of Daniel 12 *26;* of 1 Corinthians 15 *130-32;* of 1 Thessalonians 4 *94-107;* of 2 Thessalonians 2 *124-28*

Problems unresolved in posttribulationism *144-57*

Purpose of study *8*

Rapture, as a comforting hope *103-6;* contrasted to second coming *161;* exhortations in harmony with *164, 165;* Gundry on imminency of *60, 61, 70-74;* imminence of *149, 162, 163;* imminency lacking in most modern posttribulationism *33;* imminency of, in early fathers *23, 24;* lack of warning of tribulation in rapture passages *103;* partial rapture theory *7;* Payne on imminency of rapture *22;* rationale of posttribulational rapture *38;* reconciling blessed hope with post-tribulationism *57, 58;* rejection of imminency by posttribulationism *27, 70-74;* relation to endtime events *130-43;* relation to premillennialism *16, 165;* revealed to Paul *98;* silence on posttribulational rapture *161;* terminology of rapture *146;* translation, a new truth *101;* vocabulary of *48, 49;* Walvoord on rapture *22*

Reese, Alexander *17, 18, 36, 44, 89, 90, 109, 113, 120, 124, 148, 157*
Restrainer of 2 Thessalonians 2 *147*
Resurrection, first *50, 102, 147, 148*
Revelation, Book of, interpretation of *136-40, 149, 150;* Gundry's interpretation of *136-40*
Rose, George L. *35, 53*

Scripture, authority and accuracy *159*
Second chance for salvation at second coming *140, 150, 166*
Second coming of Christ, major views of *13*
Semiclassic posttribulationism *31-39;* as held by majority of posttribulationists *31;* problems of *37;* varieties of *31, 32*
Sitwell, Francis *45, 46*
Strategy of posttribulationism *7*

Theological background of posttribulationism *8, 9*
Theology, Alexandrian School of *12;* development of historically *11, 12*
Translation, not mentioned in passages on second coming *102, 103*
Tregelles, Samuel P. *43*
Tribulation, the great *148;* divine wrath in *76-79;* in semiclassic posttribulationism *34;* literal *160, 163, 164;* martyrs in, a problem to posttribulationism *79, 80;* signs of *87*

Walvoord, *The Rapture Question* *10, 159*
Wheat and tares in posttribulationism *146*
Wrath, Gundry's denial of divine wrath in great tribulation *74-80;* Gundry's view of satanic wrath *75;* minimized by posttribulationists *76;* various views on wrath in posttribulationism *54, 55*
Wuest, Kenneth S. *125*

Scripture Index

Isaiah
2 111
2:12-21 111
13:6 112
13:9-16 ....111, 112
13:11 112
13:17 112
25:6-11 25
26:19-21 26
34:1-8 ....111, 112
61:1,2 63

Jeremiah
30:7 ....64, 77
31 66
31:31-34 66

Ezekiel
20:34-38 ....100, 155

Daniel
9:24-27 40
9:27 .18, 26, 32, 34, 36, 132
12 36
12:1 ....36, 101
12:1,2 26
12:2 ....38, 101, 105, 133
12:9-12 26

Joel
1:15–2:11, 28-32 111
2:10,11 114
2:30,31 ....113, 114, 141
3:9-12 111

Amos
5:18-20 111

Obadiah
15–17 111

Zephaniah
1:7-18 ....111, 113
3:14-17 113

Zechariah
3:8,9 140
12:9–13:1 140
13:8 105
14:4,5 155

Malachi
3:1-5 140

Matthew
3:16 99

12:50 135
13 ....82, 83, 85, 87
13:30 ....83, 146
13:47-50 83
13:48-50 146
13:49,50 84
16 ....83, 86
24 ....38, 82, 88, 92, 94,
             103, 106, 162
24, 25 ....54, 80, 85,
                  145, 146
24:2 87
24:3 86
24:4-14 ....49, 87
24:15 ....77, 87, 132
24:15-22 ....36, 76
24:21 ....35, 36
24:22 77
24:27-31 154
24:29 141
24:29-31 25
24:31 ....34, 88
24:38,39,42 22
24:39 89
24:40 103
24:40, 41 ....89, 90, 146
24:41,42 90
24:42 103
24:42–25:13 26
25 ......53, 82, 84, 135, 146
25:13 22
25:31 136
25:31-46 ....58, 90, 100,
                  114, 134
25:35-39 135
27 51
27:52,53 ....51, 102

Mark
1:10 99
13:3 86
13:11 127
13:27 88
14:13 100

Luke
3:22 99
4:16-21 63
12:36-40 26
17:12 100
17:24 25
17:34-37 90
21:28 22

John
1:32,33 99

3:3-5 85
3:13 99
6:33,38,41,42,50,51,58 ..99
12:27 137
13–17 ....80, 164
14 ....92, 93, 155, 164
14:1 164
14:1-3 ....57, 80, 94, 99
14:2,3 91
14:3 ....50, 54
17:15 137
19:16 ....89, 90
21:18,19 73

Acts
1:11 26
2:17-21 112
8:1-3 35
10:11,16 99
18:9-11 73
23:11 73
24:27 73

Romans
8:18-21 25
8:19,23,25 26
11:15 26
11:26,27 140
13:11,12 109

1 Corinthians
1:7 26
1:7,8 109
1:8 119
3:13 109
5:4,5 109
5:5 119
15 ....132, 153
15:23,24 50
15:50 131
15:51 131
15:51,52 .....25, 50, 54, 66,
                  103, 131
15:51-58 ...57, 80, 94, 130,
                  153, 165
15:58 131

2 Corinthians
1:14 ....109, 119

Galatians
1:15-19 98

Philippians
1:6,10 ....109, 119
2:16 ....109, 119

3:20 26
4:5 26

1 Thessalonians
1:4 95
1:5 95
1:5,6 95
1:9 95
1:9,10 26
1:10 95
2:14 122
2:19 95
3:3-5 122
3:4 97
3:13 95
4 ....38, 94, 96, 100, 101,
103, 106, 109, 131,
149, 152, 153
4:3 95
4:8 95
4:13 115
4:13-18 ......50, 51, 54, 57,
80, 95
4:14 95
4:14-17 26
4:15 ....98, 131
4:16,17 25
4:18 165
4, 5 ....94, 96, 120, 147
5 .....55, 77, 107, 108, 109,
110, 111, 115, 116,
117, 118, 120, 155
5:1,2 116
5:1-11 80
5:2-6 26
5:3 116
5:4,5 117
5:4-6 116
5:6,7 116
5:8 117
5:8-11 116
5:9 ....78, 117
5:19 95
5:23 95

2 Thessalonians
1:3 128
1:4,5 122
1:5-10 ....122, 123
1:6-8 25
1:10 109

2 ....49, 110, 118, 147, 157
2:1 50
2:1,2 25
2:1-3 109
2:1-12 ......80, 94, 122, 124
2:3-5 125
2:5,6 97
2:6-8 126
2:8 50
3:5 122

2 Timothy
1:18 109
4:8 ....26, 109
6:14 26
6:15 22

Titus
2:11-14 57
2:12,13 ....25, 26
2:13 ....149, 165

Hebrews
8:8-13 66

James
5:7,8 26

1 Peter
1:6,7,13 26
5:4 26

2 Peter
3:12 111

Jude
1-25 38
21 26

Revelation
1–18 28
2,3 38
2:25,26 26
3:10 ....55, 137, 138
3:11 22
4–18 .....34, 38, 40, 53, 87,
103, 139, 152
4–19 162
4:1,2 136
5:8 79
5:9,10 138

6 ....76, 141
6,7 ....79, 80
6–19 149
6:7,8 114
6:8 ....78, 105
6:9-11 75
6:12 22
6:12-14 114
6:17 ....55, 76
7 ....55, 79, 80, 118
7:1-8 139
7:3 139
7:3,4 25
7:9-17 ....75, 76, 79
7:11 79
8:16 49
9:5 77
9:15 105
12:9 77
12:12 75
13:5 ....36, 77
13:7 132
13:8 85
13:8,17 133
14:1-5 139
14:3,4 25
14:9-11 ....85, 166
14:13 106
14:14-16 26
16:15 26
18 27
19 .....27, 38, 53, 100, 114,
133, 140, 141, 153
19,20 51
19–22 28
19:11-21 154
19:21 85
20 ....14, 18, 133, 156
20–22 28
20:1-6 28
20:4 ....38, 50, 51, 96, 101,
134, 153
20:4,5 25
20:4-6 ....102, 147, 148
20:10-15 28
20:11-15 135
20:12 101
20:12-14 102
21:1–22:5 28
22:7,12 22
22:20 22